I have not been able to source photographs of
Merchant Navy LSIs en-route to Normandy.
There are a few shots of them in surviving film.
The cover mock-up is intentionally ghostly!

By the same author:

Ebb and Flow, Evacuations and Landings by Merchant Ships in WW2

The first troop landing was in Norway in May 1940, promptly followed by an evacuation. Merchant ships took part in Operation Dynamo; in the next three weeks they saved over 180,000 troops and many civilians from France. Their last evacuation was from Singapore. They were involved in all the landings that followed.

The Suffolk Golding Mission, A Considerable Service.

The true story of a rescue from France in late June 1940, this may have given Ian Fleming his first idea for James Bond. It is a story of hardship and fortitude, diamonds, 'heavy water' and champagne.

With Lyle Craigie-Halkett:

Risdon Beazley, Marine Salvor.

The British salvor who managed the British salvage fleet at Normandy and thereafter. After the war the company became famous for recoveries around the world, but was largely unknown in Britain.

Merchantmen at Normandy

Roy V Martin

First published in 2017

ISBN 978-0-9557441-5-0

The last time the Merchant Navy was thought to be heroic was 70 years ago, and its limelight was brief, like the sun breaking through the clouds then gone again.

Rose George *Deep Sea and Foreign Going* 2013

Contents

Author's Note

I started on this project in 2013, then twice put it aside to concentrate on other things. Much of the original information came from the Public Record Office at Kew, more recently this has been supplemented from sources listed in the Bibliography and the text.

The best source of photographs is the Imperial War Museum, but they want £42 per photograph for permission to reproduce them for sale in the UK alone. This is way beyond my budget. The photographs I have used are not always up to the standard that Amazon require, but I have included them because I think that they are relevant.

I am grateful to Rose George for permission to reproduce the sentence from her book Deep Sea and Foreign Going.

I am most grateful to Terry Clark, a fellow Master Mariner and the editor of Southampton Master Mariners Club newsletter, for proof reading the manuscript. Terry has tried to bring my punctuation up to date using a modern grammar checker, which is 'comma rich'. Many years ago I was taught that commas were 'the spawn of the Devil' and am loath to use them generously. I have therefore followed The Economist Style Guide. The English master who made the comment about commas wrote in a report: 'if Martin ever writes one clear grammatically correct sentence I shall die a happy man.' I can't remember if he put commas in! I have not altered the punctuation when quoting others, but I have consolidated some of the one line paragraphs in the press reports.

Any mistakes are mine alone.

Roy Martin   Southampton   August 2017

Introduction

According to some sources, the British began planning their return to France 'soon after their last retreat from Dunkirk.' If you ignore the ill-fated Norwegian campaign, Dunkirk was actually Britain's first retreat of the war. When Operation Dynamo ended on 4 June the evacuation from France was little more than half complete. In the three weeks until the Armistice came into force a further quarter of a million people were rescued from France and the Channel Islands, mostly by merchant ships: more than half of those saved were from the British Expeditionary Force and British soldiers meant for the Breton Redoubt. Others included Polish and Czech troops and civilians – in many cases families of these servicemen. The operations were codenamed Cycle, from St Valery and Le Havre; then Aerial, from western France down to the Spanish border. The rescue from the Riviera coast never acquired a code name. It may have been regarded as part of Aerial, where nearly 28,000 are listed as being saved from 'unknown ports.'

After the British attacked the French fleet in Oran, the people who had been moved from Gibraltar to French controlled Morocco had to be shipped back to the U.K and elsewhere. Evacuations by sea from Greece and then Crete followed. The last, and most disastrous, retreat was from Singapore in February 1942. In all of these the merchant fleet played a significant part, saving both troops and civilians.

The fall of France greatly increased the pressure on Britain's merchant fleet, as their U-boat adversaries transferred many of their bases from Germany and Norway to the Breton Peninsular. This move reduced U-boat round trip times by about a week. The Italians established themselves at the Gironde, where their submarine base was named BETASOM. Merchant ship losses leapt from an average of sixty ships per month to ninety or more.

Worse was to come, in the first half of 1941 the average monthly loss was 115 ships. The Nation's very survival was in doubt. The Royal Air Force had successfully defended the country in the Battle of Britain and the threat of invasion had receded; now the fear was that Britain could be starved into submission.

In a letter to President Franklin D. Roosevelt, in December 1940, the Prime Minister Winston Churchill wrote:

> This mortal danger to our country is the steady and increasing diminution of our sea tonnage.
>
> We can endure the shattering of our dwellings and the slaughter of our civilian population by indiscriminate air attacks…...
>
> The decision for 1941 lies upon the seas. Unless we can establish our ability to feed this island, to import the munitions of all kinds which we need …….we may fall by the way.
>
> It is therefore in shipping and in the power to transport across the oceans, particularly the Atlantic Ocean, that in 1941 the crunch of the whole war will be found.

He later described this as the most important letter that he ever wrote.

On 6 March 1941 the Prime Minister declared that The Battle of the Atlantic was now his primary concern. His declaration was to lead to much needed improvements in the protection of convoys and faster turn rounds at the ports.

Those at sea, and ashore, were unaware of another development that would improve their fortunes. After the fall of Poland, and then France, Polish cryptographers brought with them a gift of immeasurable value – the results of their work on decoding German cyphers. To speed up the decoding the Poles had developed a machine that they called a bomba (there is no agreement on the origin of this name). Two of these were sent to the United Kingdom's main decryption establishment at Bletchley Park, where a brilliant team of specialists was already at work. What the Government Code and Cypher School lacked were the Enigma machines, and their code settings which changed each month.

In March 1941 a German naval trawler *Krebs* was captured off Norway, with two machines and the settings for the previous month. Then, in May of that year, the settings for June were captured from the German weather ship *München*. The real prize also came in May when the *U110* was boarded by a brave team from HMS *Bulldog*. Before the U-boat sank they had saved the Enigma machine, ciphers and code-books, including the important Offizier code. This operation became known as Operation Primrose: the excitement at Bletchley caused Admiral Sir Dudley Pound to signal *Bulldog* 'The petals of your flower are of rare beauty'. The reduction in merchant ship losses was immediate, between June and November they were down to fifty per month.

Worse was to come, losses in December surged to a horrifying 187 as Japan entered the war. Japan's attack on Pearl Harbour brought the Americans into the war; this was to have a decisive effect on the outcome, though it was far from immediate. In January 1942 the Germans introduced a number of changes, the most important of which was the addition of a further rotor to the U-boat Enigma machines. For the next nine months the British were, once again, unable to decode the Kriegsmarine messages.

The boarding of another damaged U-boat, by another brave naval crew, resulted in the capture of a four-rotor Enigma machine and the codebooks with all current settings for the U-boat Enigma key. This time two of the crew from HMS *Petard* lost their lives when the submarine sank; the third, a 16 year-old NAAFI assistant survived. This young man became the youngest person to be awarded the George Medal, the others were posthumously awarded the George Cross.

Again, the reduction in losses was dramatic. Baring the loss of 120 merchantmen in March 1943, those for the early part of that year averaged 61. They declined to about 30 in the second half of the year. For the rest of the war merchant ship losses were never to exceed that figure. This, and the ever-increasing supply of replacement ships from North American and British yards, meant that the build-up for the planned invasion of Europe could begin.

By September 1942 the British had completed their occupation of Madagascar. Had the Vichy French allowed the Japanese use of the island, the British would have been unable to resupply their troops in North Africa or Malta, via the Cape.

In November 1942, the Allies invaded and occupied the Vichy controlled territories of Morocco, Algeria and Tunisia, in Operation Torch. These invasions involved large numbers of British and American merchant ships, together with those from other Allies. A vast number of ships were committed to the subsequent landings in

Sicily and Italy, which took place in the second half of 1943. It was there that the first purpose built landing craft were used.

The landings in Italy had been agreed at the Casablanca conference in January 1943. At the same meeting, the heads of government of the Allies agreed to mount a mass invasion of northern Europe. Later in the year, at Tehran, it was decided that Operation Overlord (then called Round Up) would take place in May 1944. Churchill was, on the whole, less keen on the idea than Roosevelt or Stalin. Later the operations were delayed by a month to allow the Allies to strengthen their forces.

By the end of 1943 most of the convoys crossing from America included many ships and materiel for the landings. Others carried prefabricated sections of US landing craft on deck. In the same convoys sailed tugs, salvage vessels, landing craft, lake steamers and many other vessels for D-Day.

US Navy records say that even before the first Anglo-American War Conference, held in Washington 22 December 1941 – 14 January 1942, 'British Planning staffs had been at work preparing preliminary studies of the operations that would be necessary to land armies on the Continent to defeat the German forces.' However, 'In British strategy such an operation was envisaged in the final stage of the war operations in the European theatre.' The initial plans for Round Up were presented to the conference in some detail; they envisaged an invasion force leaving from south east England for somewhere in north eastern France or Belgium.

The Americans were keen to see, as fast as possible, a build-up of U.S. forces in Britain; where they could train for a full scale invasion of

Europe. The British maintained that it would be a mistake to keep British and American forces under-employed in England for at least twelve months, preferring to mount offensive operations in the Mediterranean. Perhaps it was the usual British concern about the GI's being 'over paid, over sexed and over here.'

While the two sides could not agree on any definite plan for cross-channel operations, it was agreed that the build-up of American forces would go ahead, this was code named Operation Bolero. Conscious of the need for every available merchant ship to be employed bringing in essential war materiel, fuel and troops, and with the additional task of keeping the US forces in the UK supplied; the British could not start releasing the first of their cargo ships to load for Normandy until April 1944.

Planning and Preparation

General Dwight D. Eisenhower was appointed commander of Supreme Headquarters Allied Expeditionary Force (SHAEF) in November 1943. In December General Bernard Montgomery was named as commander of the 21st Army Group, to which all of the invasion ground forces belonged, he was also given charge of developing the invasion plan. After the Tehran conference in December 1943 a Chief of Staff to the Supreme Allied Commander (Designate), COSSAC, was appointed; the plan for the invasion then became known as the COSSAC plan.

The naval operation, codenamed Neptune, was headed by Admiral Sir Bertram Ramsay RN. He assumed the title of Allied Naval Commander-in-Chief of the Allied Expeditionary Force, ANCXF, on 25 October 1943.

Admiral Ramsay's vast experience included planning the naval side of the invasion of North Africa. He went on to become the Deputy to the Allied Naval Commander-in-Chief, Admiral Sir Andrew Cunningham. After planning the naval part of the Sicilian landings, he commanded the British Task Force during that invasion. He then spent a great deal of his time, and prodigious energy, studying the problems involved in the invasion of northern France.

Frederick Leathers had been made the Minister of War Transport in 1941, when a peerage was conferred upon him. He assembled a formidable collection of shipping men, who from then on controlled every aspect of commercial shipping. For the first and only time in its history, the Merchant Navy was controlled by a unified organisation at the heart of government. It fell to them to organise every detail of the mercantile side of Operation Neptune, to meet Admiral Ramsay's requirements. Much of the detailed planning for this operation became the responsibility of Sir Ralph Metcalfe.

As at December 1943 the COSSAC plan envisaged no US naval forces being involved in Neptune. At about that time Ramsay advised the Admiralty that he would require: two Battleships, three monitors (or further battleships), 15 cruisers, 107 destroyers, 48 frigates or corvettes, 64 anti-submarine trawlers, 108 motor launches and 120 motor torpedo or motor gun boats. In addition to these 467 ships, he also planned to use almost 150 minesweepers. The Admiralty were shocked!

The arrival of General Montgomery to take over command of the British Army component of Overlord further increased the requirement. On examining the COSSAC plan Montgomery decided that the three divisional landing would result in fighting on too narrow a front; he demanded five divisions. However justified, this two-thirds increase threw an even greater burden on the ANCXF. It not only affected the number of naval ships and landing craft that would be required, it also meant a need for a proportional increase in the already staggering total of merchant ships to achieve the necessary build-up. Ramsay knew, as did Montgomery, that there was no point in landing an invasion force unless you could ensure the immediate flow of supplies that only the merchantmen could bring.

To stand some chance of meeting the new demands, D-Day was to be postponed by a month until 5 June. It was at this point that the Admiralty sought the help of the United States Navy, their Merchant Marine and the British Merchant Navy. The American component of Operation Neptune became the responsibility of Rear-Admiral Alan

Goodrich Kirk, USN. Admiral Kirk had been the United States Navy Attaché in London at the outbreak of war. One of his first wartime tasks had been to interview the Master and officers of the liner *Athenia*, which was torpedoed on the first day of the war. He and Admiral Ramsay had known one another for some years.

Admiral Ramsay knew that the operation would only succeed if it were planned in the greatest detail; but, while the Americans were used to being told what they had to do, how they would achieve the objective was largely left to their own discretion. The plans for the operation were set out in a three-inch thick foolscap book.

Even by June there would be insufficient merchant ships to carry the vehicles required for the initial assault. In peacetime, lorries (trucks) can be loaded in the tween decks of the cargo ships and, after they had been lashed, the voids could be filled with baled goods and the like. To do this would have meant a delay in discharge, but without the baled goods, each lorry occupied a space as big as its extreme measurements. This problem did not occur with the landing craft as they were designed for drive-on drive-off operation; but even the vast number of larger landing craft who could ship the lorries would not be able to carry a sufficient number. Each Liberty ship and its equivalent could carry 120 lorries and 480 troops; twelve British Mk III landing craft would be required to equal this.

Montgomery had to agree that the number of lorries could be reduced from 3,200 to 2,500 per division. Even this meant shipping nearly 3,000 more of these space hungry beasts, together with drivers, mechanics, and petrol. The General also had to accept a reduction in the number of landing craft that were to have been modified as gunships, so that they could carry some of the extra vehicles.

To ease the burden that the change would impose on Admiral Ramsay; Rear-Admiral Sir Philip Vain was appointed to take command of the British Task Force, while it was at sea.

The substantial revision of the Combined Planning was begun on 14 January 1944; though not all the parties involved had had time to agree to the changes. It was not until 7 February that American agreement was received; in some accounts, the Americans were said to have been most unhappy. Even when all had accepted the changes, it was not before 20 March that the additional ships had been identified. They had to be diverted from other tasks and, in some cases, mobilised over long distances, putting considerable extra strain on convoy organisation.

There was not only a shortage of ships and landing craft; there was an even greater shortage of tugs to move the two Mulberry harbours. Added to this were shortages of loading berths and lighterage at the ports. In many cases it was thought that there would need to be partial or complete crew changes, to ensure that only those who had volunteered would be signed on the extra vessels.

Fortunately the merchant service had risen to the occasion and over 32,000 men, and at least one woman, had volunteered for the task. This was in addition to the many already serving on specialized units such as tugs and salvage vessels. A press release at the time of the invasion says that 50,000 manned one thousand ships. Many merchant seamen serving elsewhere at that time were not even aware that volunteers had been sought.

In the opening sentence of his orders for Operation Neptune Admiral Ramsay summed up his task as: 'the safe and timely arrival of the assault forces at their beaches, the cover of their landings, and subsequently the support and maintenance and the rapid build-up of our forces ashore.' The phrase 'the safe and timely arrival' had been first used in summarizing the Royal Navy's duties with regard to convoys.

Meanwhile the Admiralty continued to pressure the Admiral to reduce his naval requirements; which, fortunately for the success of the mission, he refused to do. In fact ,he put his faith in the willingness of the United States to participate; he was not disappointed. That said the British Royal and Merchant Navies still provided more than three quarters of the eventual fleet. The total combined naval contribution now was:

Six (two) Battleships, two (three) monitors, 22 (15) cruisers, 119 (107) destroyers, 113 (48) sloops, frigates or corvettes, 80 (64) anti-submarine trawlers, patrol craft and gunboats, 360 (108) motor launches and 120 motor torpedo or motor gun boats and American PT boats. His original requests are shown in brackets. This gave a total of 702 (467) warships; in addition the number of minesweepers had increased from 12 to 25 flotillas. Winser also lists eleven and 'a squadron'; with all the motor minesweepers and magnetic mine sweepers, he has a total of 307 craft.

The provision and control of the merchant ships was the responsibility of the Ministry of War Transport, MOWT. They had to provide the necessary ships, while maintaining seaborne traffic throughout the world and deal with a wide range of other bodies. The most obvious of these were the railway companies and harbour authorities. In many instances the ports and railway owners were one and the same, but the mighty ports in the Thames, the Mersey and the

Clyde were owned by separate organisations. All of the ports had been targets of the Luftwaffe and had suffered a great deal of damage. Cargoes were also brought to the docks by road and canal.

Demands for equipment and supplies had to be met, without affecting the war effort elsewhere on land, sea and air. Food still needed to be imported and distributed; fuel supplies, mostly coal, were maintained. Labour had to be directed to where it was required. Areas of the country and coast had to be cleared by evacuating their populations so that training could take place and temporary embarkation points established. All this, and much more, was achieved without computers. That last sentence needs to be qualified, of course. Bletchley Park had the use of the GPO (General Post Office), built Colossus One computer. The improved version, Colossus Two, came into operation just in time for the landings. The very existence of the world's first electronic computer was a closely guarded secret and its use confined to decoding high-level enemy signal traffic.

There could be no question of having all of the troops and supplies close to their loading site; to do so would have caused bottlenecks and left the concentrations even more vulnerable to attack by the enemy. There was also the problem of alerting the German reconnaissance aircraft. So, troops and supplies were hidden, as much as possible, often far from the loading ports until needed. These 'dumps' were all over southern England, as much as sixty miles inland, and troops and their vehicles were hidden in woods and on common land.

Similarly, too many loaded ships lying at anchor would attract unwanted attention; but it was essential that sufficient materiel be preloaded to meet all the requirements of the assault phase. Almost 300 ships had been selected as Mechanised Transport ships (elsewhere named Motor Transport or Military Transport ships). As previously stated the primary function of many was to carry 480 men and 120 vehicles. Other cargoes included petrol (gas), spares, and rations. These ships came, in equal numbers, from the Americans and the British. Bulk oil tankers were also employed to ship petrol and water.

Staff at the Ministry of War Transport and its US equivalent drew up plans for cargo stowage on the MT vessels, so that each ship would have similar combinations of cargo for the assault phase. They were aided by the fact that a large proportion of the cargo ships were of similar size and layout, 10,000 tons deadweight (carrying capacity). The loss of a ship, or ships, would not leave the forces on the Far Shore short of any one commodity and ships could be discharged on arrival. This became known as 'balanced loading'. The idea being that the ships that survived a particularly hazardous journey, such as the ones to besieged Malta, would bring at least a percentage of all the desperately needed supplies. Balanced loading had then been used for landings in the Mediterranean. One source says that that idea was the result of bitter experience in the Norwegian campaign of 1940, where our troops were enduring almost continual attack from the air. In one instance, desperately needed anti-aircraft guns were delivered, but the ship carrying the ammunition had been sunk.

Balanced loading was not an option for those tasked with loading the coasters. Coasters were small ships that normally traded around the coasts of the UK and, in peacetime, from the Elbe to Brest. They were as varied as the trades they were designed for and the particular requirements of their owners. In size, they varied from 200 to 2,000 tons deadweight. In all, nearly 500 were made available for the operation. Of these 184 were allocated to the Americans, who chartered a number of Dutch schuyts as well. These little Dutch ships were used to making their way into the smallest of ports at high tide, often sitting on the bottom as the ports dried out. This made them most useful in landing cargoes at the smaller Normandy ports. Even they were initially far from keen on beaching on a shelving sand shore, with rock outcrops, especially under gunfire! This was soon overcome and most of the coasters beached where they could be discharged into DUKWs. The first 69 coasters arrived at Seine Bay on the afternoon of D-Day.

Loading the coasters was governed by the amount of cargo they could carry, with the additional requirement that the most needed cargo should to be stowed last, near the top of the hold from where it could be removed first. So if a ship had a cargo that would take three days to discharge, the cargo required to be in France on day one would be the last to be loaded in the UK. Though the cargo for day three loading was not always alongside when the ship arrived. Also, the desire of the various supply services to maximize the use of available tonnage sometimes led to ships being overloaded and less than essential cargo being delivered. One example was a shipment that included razor blades and grass seed!

Two organisations were set up to reduce possible delays to a minimum. One was the 'Build-up and Control Organisation' (BUCO), and the other the 'Turn-round Control Organisation' (TURCO). TURCO's task was to control the routeing of ships to and from ports where berths and cargoes were waiting, combine the ships into convoys, and clear ships that had discharged from the beachhead as soon as possible. BUCO matched military needs with available shipping.

Admiral Ramsay insisted on three principles: The most immediate was to land the maximum military force and the maximum amount of stores and equipment in the first three days. The next was the 'Build-up' after D+3, with a regular schedule of daily convoys from each of the loading ports, avoiding alternating peaks and troughs in the arrival of materiel. The third concerned the operation of the various classes of landing craft; where possible these were to use the same port and berth for each visit. A repeating three-day timetable was to be kept to.

Every ship was to carry an identifying number on each side of the bridge or centre castle, with space below to indicate which convoy she belonged to on that particular trip. For example, the cargo ship *Empire Farmer*, MT51, left the Thames in convoy ETM7, the seventh MT convoy in the series from England, Thames. The ETA at Sword Beach was 13 June. On her return, the ship would have been in a convoy with the first letter F, for France, and the second letter the destination, say W for the Solent (Isle of Wight). Some photographs of ships show them flying the signal letter M, followed by pennants showing their MT number.

Landing tables for the LCAs that were on the LSI(L)s were prepared in March. These documented those ranks that were to be on each numbered LCA. 'Trux' has listed the modified tables for Sword on: http://ww2talk.com/forums/topic/38764-sword-beach/page-3?hl=sword, and subsequent pages. Elsewhere on the site, he has provided detailed information for the other British and Canadian beaches. He is now (April 2017), posting data for Omaha.

Merchant Ships taking part in NEPTUNE (from US sources) were:

Personnel Ships and LSIs. (?)	18
M.T. Ships	224
M.T. Coasters	64
Store Coasters	122
Tankers & Colliers	150
Cased Petrol Carriers	136
Blockships	55
Ammunition Carriers	76
Ammunition Supply Issuing Ships (ASIS)	18
Liberty Store Ships	78
Hospital Ships and Carriers	10
Accommodation Ships	10
Miscellaneous, 225 tugs & 39 salvage vessels?	295
TOTAL MERCHANT SHIPS	**1256**
TOTAL LANDING SHIPS & CRAFT	**3978**
TOTAL NAVAL FORCES	**1089**
GRAND TOTAL	**6346**

John de S Winser lists 77 Assault, Troop and Attack Ships/Transports (of which 40 were British Merchant ships); 326 Military Stores Ships, 415 Coasters, 237 Tank Landing Ships and 1,464 Assault Landing Craft. 1,633 Naval Craft of all types and 863 other vessels. This gives a total of 5,015 self-propelled ships involved in the landings. I believe this figure to be correct, with the balance of LCAs and other small craft being carried there by larger ships.

The Assault Ships

There were several classes of vessels employed as assault and troop ships. Out of the total of 77, the United States provided 20, the Royal Navy 16, plus 5 Headquarters ships; the balance remained with the Merchant Navy and the US Merchant Marine. Thus, the Merchant Navy manned just over half of all the Assault ships that carried the infantry to Normandy at dawn on D-Day. These were affectionately known to the Canadians, and probably others, as 'mother ships.'

The 40 British merchant vessels came from several sources. Many had been packet ships, what would now be called ferries. The bulk of the packets were owned by the various railway companies. Two small ferries came from the United States and three had been British passenger liners. Another 13 had been built for the MOWT in America on Lend/Lease; these had been modified while under construction. A number of passenger liners and two packets acted as troop ships, and many of the MT ships and coasters carried troops and their vehicles.

The 13 US built ships were modified C1-S-AY type Victory Ships. All were Red Ensign ships at D-Day. They were built by the Consolidated Steel Corporation of Wilmington, California, and bareboat chartered to the Ministry of War Transport. All were 7,177 grt. 11,650 tons dwt, 417 feet long and had a top speed of 14 knots. This class carried 1,310 troops. Newspaper reports say that the modifications were thought up by the MOWT. It is more likely that they were a variant of the Victory ship, which had been evolved at the pre-war design stage.

The ships were manned by a normal wartime Merchant Navy complement of about 80. For example the *Empire Spearhead* had a Master, Captain Hill, three deck officers, plus a Purser/Troop officer, later a Fourth Officer was engaged as a Troop Officer. The Boatswain was in charge of a deck department of 12. The Chief Engineer had six engineers and two electricians. There were 12 engine room ratings, plus a Winchman, a Plumber and a Storekeeper.

The biggest increase was in the catering department, where the Chief Steward was responsible for 20 stewards, seven cooks and four bakers. The three (MN), Radio Officers had been on a week's signal course to prepare for the task.

In addition, a naval officer was the Senior Naval Officer Transport SNO(T), or SNOT, as you prefer. Other naval personnel included: four to man each assault craft, a number of signalmen, known in the navy as 'bunting tossers', plus medics.

The merchant LSIs carried 18 DEMS gunners, short for Defence Equipped Merchant Ships. On the LSIs the DEMS gunners were naval ratings. On other merchant ships they also came from a special section of the Royal Artillery,; many ships having both soldiers and naval seamen at the same time. The ship's crew, particularly the Apprentices, when they were carried, helped with handling the ammunition.

Nine of the LSIs were transferred to the Navy between the end of June and September 1944.

Ship	Official No	Group	Manager
Empire Anvil	169768	550	Blue Star Line
Empire Arquebus	169819	524	Donaldson Bros & Black
Empire Battleaxe	169703	537	Cunard White Star

Empire Broadsword	169737	538	Cunard White Star
Empire Crossbow	169808	553	Peninsular and Oriental
Empire Cutlass	169740	536	Canadian Pacific
Empire Gauntlet	169807	552	Ellerman City Line
Empire Halberd	169695	539	Furness Withy
Empire Javelin	169774	551	Blue Star Line
Empire Lance	169742	540	Canadian Pacific
Empire Mace	169752	541	Anchor Line
Empire Rapier	169757	542	Furness Withy
Empire Spearhead	169773	525	Royal Mail Lines

All carried 18 LCAs, except *Empire Halberd* 16 + 2 LCOCUs and *Empire Lance* which had one LCOCU and 17 LCAs. LCOCU were Obstruction Clearance Units, which were able to carry divers and their gear.

The Combined Operations Pamphlet No 11, about Landing Ships Infantry, contains only two references to Red Ensign LSIs; one outlines the desirability of having a separate troop deck for the naval parties and the other the duties of the SNO(T).

Other British Merchant ocean-going ships serving as LSIs, also with Merchant Navy crews, were:

| *Clan Lamont* | 7,526 | Clan Line |
| *Llangibby Castle* | 11,951 | Union Castle |

| *Monowai* (NZ) | 10,852 | Union Steamship | |
| *Pampas* | 8,244 | Royal Mail | (Reserve) |

The Packets were mostly capable of steaming at more than 20 knots. They were each equipped with six Landing Craft Assault (LCA), craft and most carried over four hundred troops. They were:

Red Ensign ships

Amsterdam	4,220	London North Eastern Railway
Ben-my-Chree	2,586	Isle of Man Steam Packet
Biarritz	2,388	Southern Railway
Canterbury	2,910	Southern Railway
Duke of Argyll	3,814	London Midland & Scottish Rail
Isle of Guernsey	2,143	Southern Railway
Isle of Thanet	2,701	Southern Railway
Lady of Mann	3,104	Isle of Man Steam Packet
Lairds Isle	1,783	Burns & Laird
Maid of Orleans	2,386	Southern Railway
Meckleburg	2,907	Dutch Mail, Zeeland (Dutch Flag)
Princess Margaret	2,552	London Midland & Scottish Rail
Princess Maud	2,883	London Midland & Scottish Rail
St Helier	1,952	Great Western Railway

Victoria	1,641	Isle of Man Steam Packet

White Ensign ships

		Owner
Brigadier	2,294	Southern Railway *Worthing*
Duke of Wellington	3,743	London Midland & Scottish Rly
Glenearn	9,784	Glen Line (Holt) – cargo liner
Glenroy	9,809	Glen Line (Holt) – cargo liner
Invicta	4,178	Southern Railway
Prince Baudouin	3,219	Belgian State Railways
Prince Charles	3,950	Belgian State Railways
Prince David	6,892	Canadian National as HMCS
Prince Henry	6,893	Canadian National as HMCS
Prince Leopold	2,950	Belgian State Railways
Prins Albert	2,938	Belgian State Railways
Prinses Astrid	2,950	Belgian State Railways
Prinses Josephine Charlotte	2,950	Belgian State Railways
Queen Emma	4,135	Dutch Mail, Zeeland *Koningin Emma*
Royal Ulsterman	3,244	Burns & Laird
Ulster Monarch	3,791	Belfast Steamship Company

The Hospital Carriers

These smaller vessels were adapted to transport casualties; again, several were packets. Most were to discharge their patients at the Outer Dock at Southampton, the peacetime base for the Southern Railway packets to France and the Channel Islands. Outer Dock had the advantage that it had rail lines alongside the berths, it was also close to the Southampton Terminus Station. The dock is now called Ocean Village.

From Southampton casualties were dispersed all over the south of England, many to country houses that had been converted into hospitals. A least one of these hospitals was close to Weymouth, which also had a railway running along the dock. This does not seem to have been used for this purpose, unless the Americans landed their injured there. The writer remembers the slow moving hospital trains which came from the Southampton direction.

All but one of the ships carried six landing craft adapted as 'water ambulances'. The Medical Staff were provided by the Royal Army Medical Corp or the United States Army; depending on which task force they served. In addition to transporting casualties, the ships were effectively floating Accident and Emergency centres. All but the Dutch flagged *Batavier II* were Red Ensign ships. They were painted white, with a broad green band broken at three points to allow red crosses to be inserted. An identifying number was painted on bow and quarter. Like all approved hospital vessels they were supposedly exempt from attack, but, as the Allies had found during the Mediterranean landings, the Luftwaffe failed to observe their status and some were sunk. Also, sea mines failed to differentiate between them and other targets.

Batavier II had been converted in London to be Hospital Carrier No 50; with accommodation for 215 patients. After training in the Thames Estuary she sailed for Southampton on 6 June. From there she was due to sail to Gold on the 7 June, but was inexplicably prevented from doing so because of 'shortage of coal'. This delayed the sailing until the 11th, when she was unable to find her convoy. She was returning to the Solent when she met the outbound convoy. On the far shore she embarked 198 casualties, just over half being stretcher cases. When the northbound convoy was attacked, she escaped damage.

On 11 June, the *Batavier II* was instructed to sail just as the 'Great Storm' was starting. Because of the high seas, her water ambulances could not be launched and she again ran low on coal and returned empty. At Southampton a severe leak had to be repaired; later she was in collision with three American vessels while anchored off Cherbourg. Not a lucky ship!

The Southern Railway's *Dinard* No 28 was no more fortunate to begin with. She sailed for Juno on the 7 June, but did not keep to the swept channel and struck a mine that evening. There were doubts as to whether the casualty would founder and the order was given to abandon ship. Two naval trawlers got her back to the Isle of Wight, from where, with extra pumps, she made Southampton. The ship was under repair until the 17 June, when she embarked her first 236 off Juno. After that poor start she made frequent successful crossings.

The London Midland and Scottish Railway's *Duke of Lancaster* was fitted out as Hospital Carrier No 56. Her first sailing was on the 8

June. She returned with 245 casualties, including 42 POWs. On her return she was diverted to Portsmouth, as all the Southampton berths were occupied. This ship was also twice delayed by bunker and water shortages. It should be said that these vessels were designed to make short passages and probably had small bunker spaces.

Another LMS ship, the *Duke of Rothesay*, became Hospital Carrier 62. Her first sailing for Juno was on 8 June. She loaded off several beaches, returning with 315 wounded and two dead servicemen. In fair weather it was found that the water ambulances were successful in transporting casualties over comparatively short distances. Their record was ferrying 115 cases, in two hours, while the ship was anchored three miles off. On 30 June this ship embarked five hundred casualties, including 334 stretcher cases, 111 more than her rated capacity.

The Coast Line ship *Lady Connaught*, Hospital Carrier No 55, was allocated to the US Utah Beach. Her Medics were therefore provided by the Americans. Her capacities were 95 stretcher patients and 246 walking wounded; but on her first sailing on 9 June, she carried a total of 450 injured. She maintained an uninterrupted service throughout the month of June and beyond.

The *Naushon* and the *New Bedford* were two ferries that had been built by the Bethlehem Ship Building Corporation of Quincy, Mass. The *New Bedford* was only two hundred feet long; getting her across the Atlantic was an achievement in itself. Both were put under the Red Ensign and allocated the US Western Task Force, arriving at Omaha Beach on 8 June.

The London North Eastern Railway ship *Prague* was the fourth ship for the two Western Task Force beaches. She was designated Hospital Carrier No 51. She made her first crossing on 7 June and maintained a regular service to the beaches, followed by Cherbourg and Dieppe. The *Prague* was equipped to treat and transport 194 stretcher cases and 228 walking wounded.

The US war correspondent Martha Gellhorn was probably on the *Prague*; whichever of the four ships she sailed on we are indebted to her for a description of, among other things, the merchant crews. It is difficult to believe that she boarded without active help from members of the crew. She said that she only came out of the lavatory that she had been hiding in, when she heard the ships engines start. If so she could still have been disembarked, but fortunately she wasn't.

Her stepson, Sandy Matthews[i], handles her Estate, he lives near Torquay. He has not responded to a message I sent, so I cannot quote extensively from her dispatch without infringing copyright. I will therefore paraphrase some of her report. An online search will find at least an abridged version of the article.

She confirms that there were 422 beds on the ship, which ties in with the *Prague*. There were six nurses, who had been training in the USA up to three weeks before. They had been allocated to a railway train ambulance, but found themselves on a ship – something that they didn't seem to have complained about. The 'beautifully white' hospital carrier sailed alone, with 'not so much as a pistol on board.' She says that they crossed in daylight and it seemed a long morning and the captain never left the bridge as they made their way through the mine-swept channel.

She confirms that they had six water ambulances 'light motor launches that swung down from the ship's side and could be raised the same way when full of wounded.' She describes the orders being given to the civilian boats crews, as they set off with their American stretcher-bearers. Upon return, 'the ship's crew became volunteer stretcher bearers instantly.' The four doctors, six nurses, and about 14 medical orderlies had to be great people to care for 400 wounded men. She describes the sterling work of these Americans in detail.

Somehow or other she managed to get ashore on one of the water ambulances. Once there they were stuck for some time on a falling tide. It was long dark before they assembled the injured on a British LCT. 'The night too; went on longer than other nights. Our water ambulances found us and there was a lot of incomprehensible cockney talk among the boatmen.' The stretcher-bearers had realised on the LCT that most of their casualties were German; but all did their duty, as always. With more cockney chat, they set off. 'So, full of conversation, we zigzagged back to the ship and were at last swung aboard.'

Everyone was waiting for daylight, everyone longing for England. They had faith in their ship and 'counted on one another'. All, 'from the British captain to the London messboy, did his job tirelessly well.' Similarly 'the doctors, nurses and orderlies were there for the wounded and the wounded alone, and would not fail them.' Then the coast came in sight and English air flowed through the wards and the wounded seemed to feel it. The captain shouted down from the bridge, "Look at it! Just look at it!" 'He had spoken for all of us.'

US sources give the medical complement as five officers, five nurses, and 49 enlisted men. British manning was similar with the Officers,

NCOs and other ranks coming from the Royal Army Medical Corps and the Matron and five nursing sisters from the Queen Alexandra's Imperial Military Nursing Service (as it was until 1949).

All of the ship and boats crews were merchant seamen. What is not clear is where the extra civilian boatmen were recruited. They may have been from the ships' home ports; London in the case of the *Prague* – hence all the cockney chat.

Like the Merchant Infantry Landing ships, these ships have been largely forgotten; any occasional reference being incorrectly prefixed HMHS.

The Cargo Ships

In 1939 the British merchant fleet was still the largest in the World, with about 3,000 ocean going vessels and over one thousand coasters. Many of the ships were old and a substantial proportion had been laid-up during the depression. Shipyards that had closed down in the 1930s were reactivated, but Britain needed more new buildings than the yards could supply.

Prime Minister Winston Churchill realised early on that the U-boats would starve the country into submission unless losses could be replaced. British yards alone could not achieve the required replacement rate.

Mr Cyril Thompson, the joint Managing Director of the ship builders J L Thompson, headed up a British Shipbuilding Mission to the USA. He was accompanied by Mr Harry Hunter, the Technical Director of the engine builder North Eastern Marine. They crossed the Atlantic on the Cunard liner *Scythia* in September 1940; with the plans of their ship, the *Dorington Court.* In New York they were joined by Mr Bill Bennett and Mr Stuart Heck, both Principal Surveyors of Lloyds Register and Mr R R Powell, a British Admiralty representative.

Their intention was to buy sixty ships similar to the *Dorington Court.* No up-to-date ships of this size could be had in the USA, so they set off to tour the main ship building yards in North America. No building ways were free either. The Mission's task then changed to building two shipyards from scratch. One of the many problems was finding an engineering firm who could manufacture Scotch boilers required for the ships; the Americans having given these up in favour of water tube boilers. The problem was solved by placing the order with locomotive manufacturers, who still produced this older type of smoke tube boilers.

Contracts for the ships were signed on 20 December 1940. The new yards were in Portland, Maine and Richmond, California. Once the sixty ships were delivered the British were able to sell the two yards back to the Americans; later these yards delivered 374 Liberty ships between them.

The Mission also ordered 26 ships in Canada, to the same design; there ,they were called the North Sands type after one of the Thompson UK yards. During the war the Canadians built just over 350 ships of these ships, which they named Forts and Parks. The Forts being for the British and the Parks to sail under the Canadian flag.

His task complete, Thompson returned to the UK on the *Western Prince*. He was one of the survivors when the ship was torpedoed and sunk on 14 December 1940. He and his valuable papers were picked up nine hours later by the *Baron Kinnard*. This tramp steamer had already played an important part in Operation Aerial; rescuing about two thousand people from St Jean de Luz, as the Armistice came into force.

Back in their Sunderland yard, Thompson's built 23 tramps to their own design; nine with the same dimensions as the *Empire Liberty,* an improved version of the *Dorington Court*. The beam had been reduced by three feet and the bilge radius increased to allow a longer mid-body.

Early in 1941, the Americans were realising that they would need to expand their merchant fleet; Admiral Land was put in charge of the programme. He regarded the Ocean class as far too slow for the task, and wanted a new design. The naval architects, Gibbs and Cox, persuaded the Admiral that there would be insufficient time to prepare a new design, and recommended that the *Empire Liberty* specification should be used.

A number of modifications were made in the United States. Steam was to be provided by two oil fired water tube boilers; the hull plates were to be welded rather than riveted and, most obviously, the accommodation block was combined in one superstructure amidships. The differences in British and American design practice showed up. The British drawing offices produced a total of about fifty plans for a new build, while Gibbs and Cox had to draw ten times that number. One positive result was that parts and spares for a Liberty ship were always interchangeable.

In June 1941 Robert Cyril Thompson was made an OBE, and later maybe a CBE: either way a rather miserly award for a man who had given the Allies the most famous standard ship of all time. Well over 3,000 variants of the *Empire Liberty* were launched. Of these 216 Liberties, 36 Forts and eleven Oceans were allocated to Operation Neptune.

In 1943 Thompson joined the RAF as a non-commissioned flight mechanic, becoming a Pilot Officer towards the end of the war. He was only 59 when he died of a heart attack on 9 March 1967.

John W. Brown, **as a limited capacity troop ship, courtesy ABS
This ship was not at Normandy, but is similar to many that were.
She is preserved in the United States.**

The newly built *Ocean Liberty* goes to war   **Courtesy ABS**

Name	Built	GRT	NRT	LOA	Beam	Depth	IHP	Fuel
Embassage	1935	4954	2912	409.2	57.6	24.0	353	Coal
Dorington Court	1939	5281	3113	426.0	59.9	25.5	420	Coal
Empire Liberty	1941	7157	4284	423.8	57.2	34.9	520	Coal
Ocean Vanguard.	1941	7174	4272	425.1	57.0	34.8	505	Coal
Sambut .	1943	7191	4380	423	57.0	34.8	339?	Oil
Fort Tadoussac	1941	7129	4259	424.5	57.2	34.9	505	Coal

Sambut was one of a number of Liberties delivered to the British. All had triple expansion steam engines. The last four were delivered as Closed Shelter Deck (CSD), or full scantling ships. A CSD ship's freeboard is measured from the weather deck, while an Open Shelter Deck ships freeboard deck is the tween deck. Early in the war, existing OSD had their shelter decks closed to increase their carrying capacity.

In the British ships, accommodation for the gunners and, in some cases, the Commodore's staff, was in number five tween deck. The ship's funnels were tall and thin to allow for natural draft to the boilers. A forced draft ship would have had a shorter broader funnel. Seamen often refer to a plump female as 'a forced draft job.' At first sight the Liberties had the shorter funnel; but the flue length, through the accommodation, was the same. These funnels and their masts and derricks differentiate cargo ships from warships.

The Oceans, Forts, and Parks were built to the basic North Sands specification. Every possible saving was made in these ships, most did not have running water, or plumbed wastes, in the officers wash basins, or the baths. For all crew, water was heated by pumping up fresh water, often by hand, and then heating it with a piece of rubber hose connected to a steam pipe, a hazardous exercise! Brocklebank, a liner company, had the *Fort Ville Marie* in their fleet, where she was known as the 'Vile Mary'. As time went by, the Canadians made a number of improvements and the later ships were delivered as 'Canadian Victory' ships.

Most British shipyards had designed similar classes of vessels. Another variant was a diesel ship, with a three-cylinder Doxford opposed piston engine, giving ten knots on less than ten tons of diesel oil per day. The Doxford shipyards version was known as the Economy Doxford. These basic ships had Scotch boilers to run their cargo winches and auxiliaries. By 1941, an Improved Economy Doxford was introduced and, as far as the crews were concerned, they were much in need of improvement.

Many of the designs were built for shipping companies, even during the war; many more were completed for the Ministry of War Transport. The following drawings show the evolution of the class:

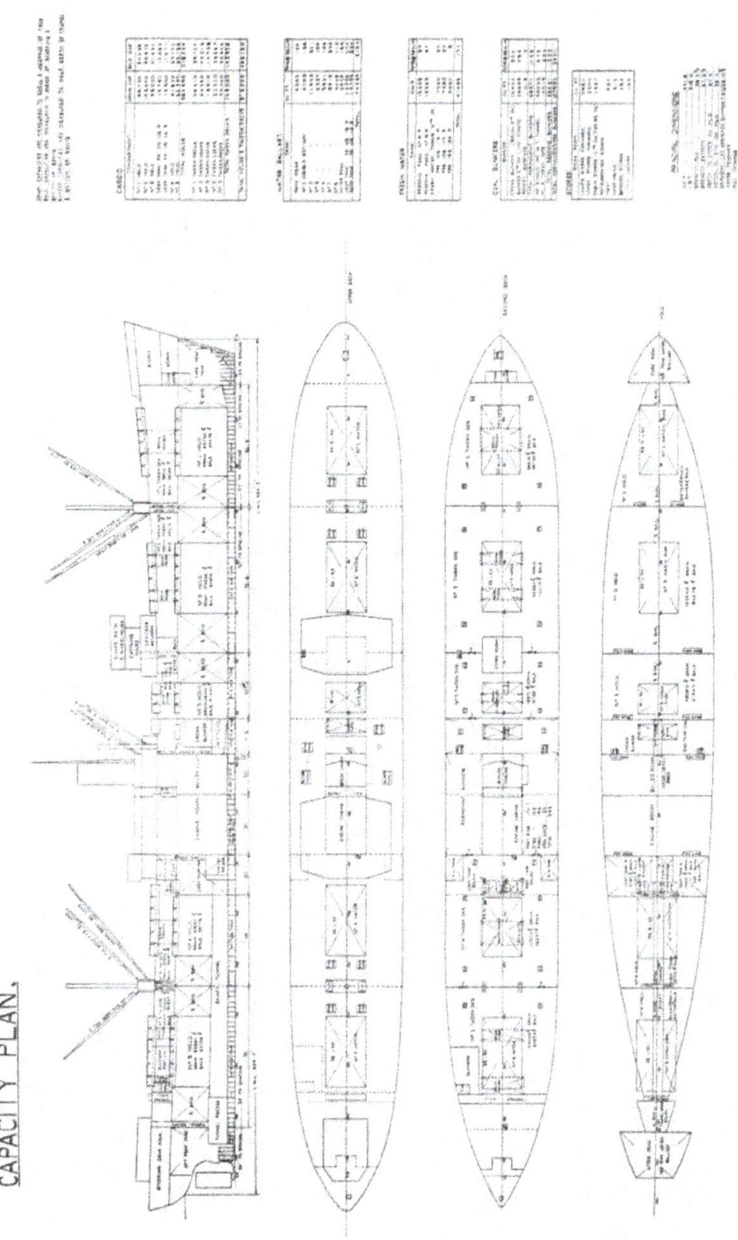

The Ocean Class   **Courtesy ABS**

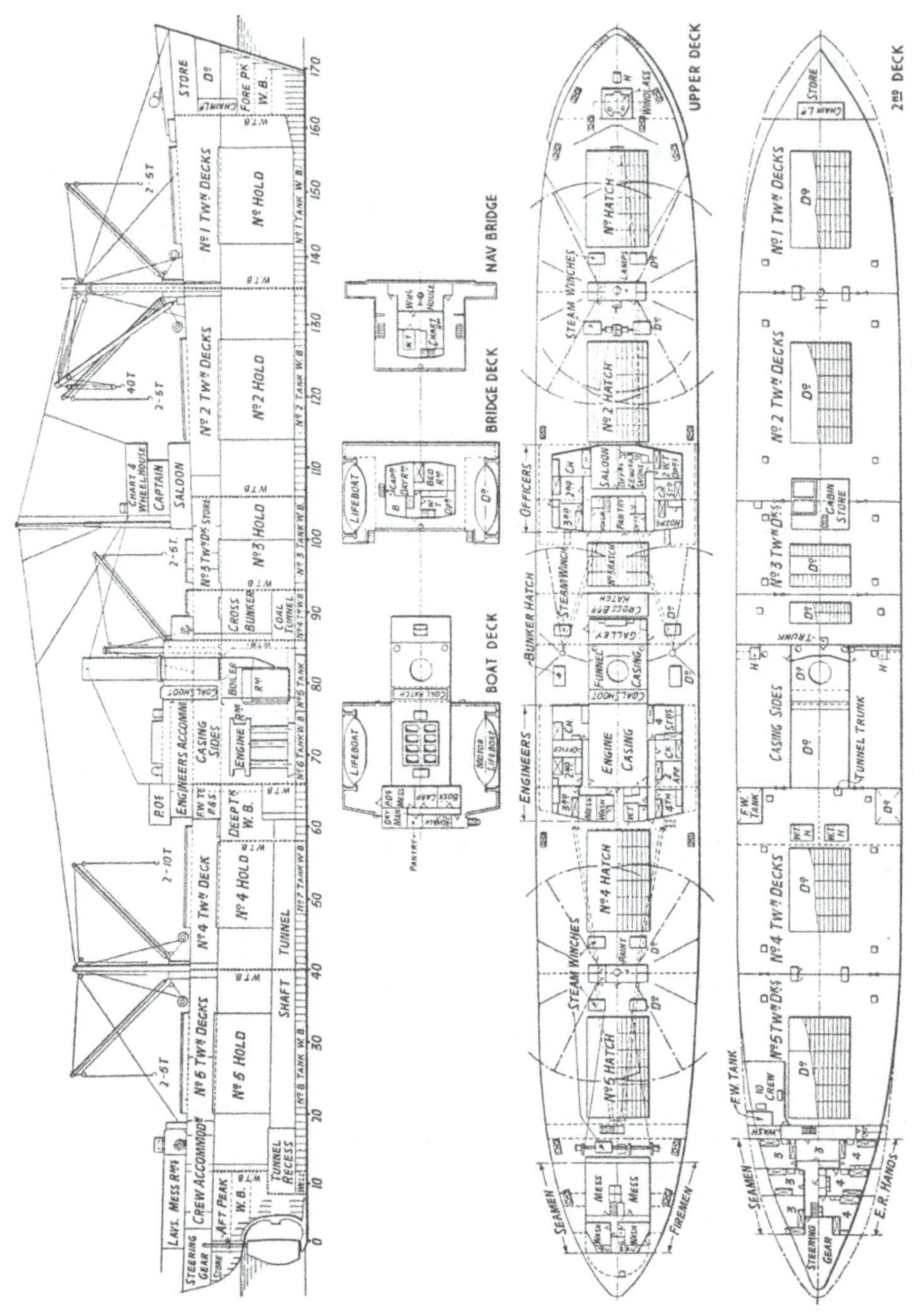

The *Empire Liberty*   **Courtesy ABS**

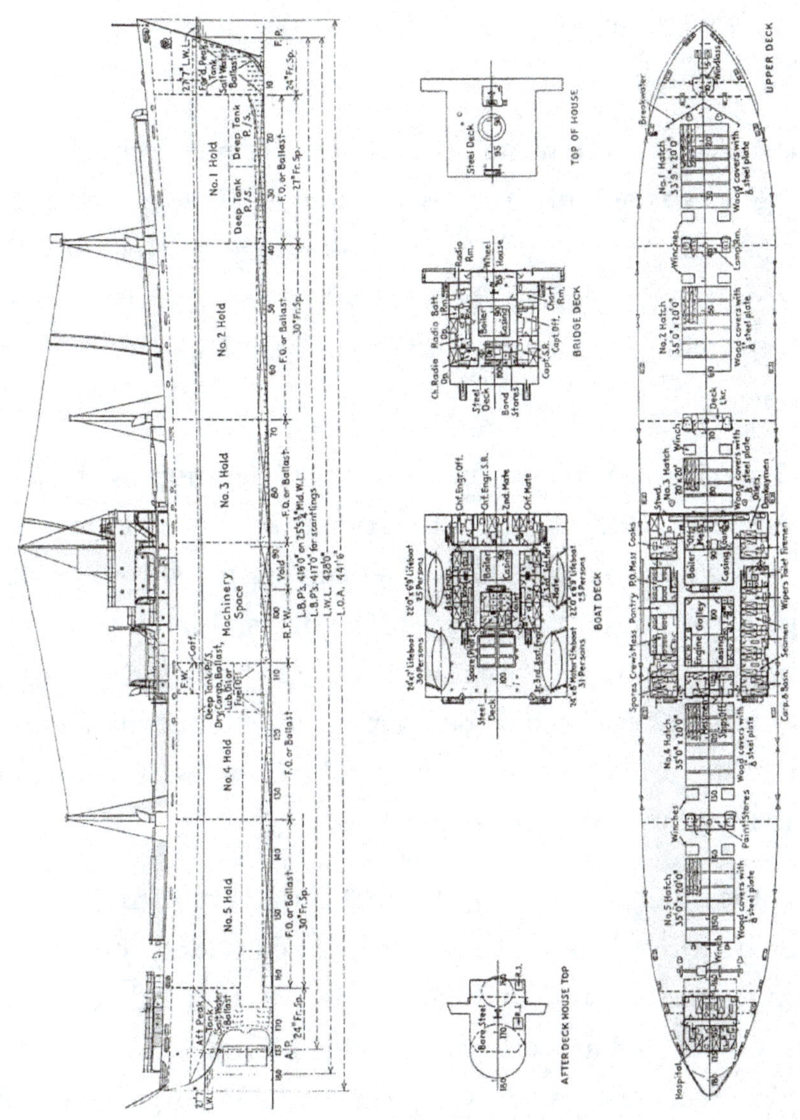

The Liberty   **Courtesy ABS**

Many smaller vessels, such as the 31 N3 coasters (popularly known as Jeeps), and T1-M-BT1/2 coastal tankers, were built in America. These and others were sailed across the wild Atlantic by British crews in time for the landings.

The N3-S-A1 design was developed at the request of the British to replace lost coastal tonnage. These ships could be built in the smaller yards, including those in the Great Lakes where access was limited by the size of the canal locks. These vessels were typical three-island, two deck ships with poop, bridge deck and forecastle and two hatches in each well.

The N3-S-A1 was a coal-burner, ideal for operation by the British. The N3-S-A2 version was oil fired, otherwise the dimensions were similar. Both classes were named after American clipper ship-masters and were provided under Lend-Lease. The British built a similar vessel, the Scandinavian type. Both classes were to be found on the short sea trades for many years after the war; as were the German equivalent, known to the British as Hansa boats. The Canadians also built 27 ships to the Scandinavian design.

Among the other types of coaster that proved particularly useful was the Dutch Schuyt. These little vessels varied widely, but they were all diesel powered and mostly had a loaded draft of only eight feet, 2.5 meters. Of the 50 that were employed at Normandy almost half were in American service transhipping cargoes from larger ships for discharge in the small river ports.

The Tugs

During the latter part of the 18th century, the Scot James Watt, had greatly improved the efficiency of the Newcomen steam engine. He went into partnership with Matthew Boulton in Birmingham gaining access to a precision engineering works. This eventually made his engine, with a separate condenser, a viable means of propulsion. The first practical steam tug was the *Charlotte Dundas*, built in 1802; this vessel was designed by another Scots engineer, William Symington and funded by Lord Dundas. The tug was used to make a few barge tows on local rivers and the Firth and Clyde canal, but encountered opposition from many vested interests. In the USA Robert Fulton built the North River Steamboat in 1807, again using a Watt engine.

In 1816 the British paddle steamer *Defiance* became the first steamer to enter Dutch waters. When the Dutch bought the tiny British steam tug *Monarch* in 1825, the British already had some years of towing experience. All realised that the new steam tugs could be used to tow sailing ships up river to port; a process that had, until then, taken many days.

As the size and reliability of the engines and boilers improved, and the vessels were capable of going to sea, they began to steam further to meet the incoming sailing vessels. This trade became known as 'seeking': it was only a small step to assisting disabled ships.

When the Dutch realised that tugs could be used to tow dredgers and barges over long distances, they gained an advantage in that trade that they did not lose until very recently. These same tugs, when returning from delivering their tows, became the first true deep-sea rescue tugs. With the increase in the use of steam for propulsion of ocean-going ships, the results from 'seeking' declined and most of the UK commercial tug owners pulled out of the business.

By the First World War, the British had few truly sea-going tugs and those that they did have had an endurance of a few days. The Admiralty realised that the only practical solution was to design, build and operate suitable tonnage. Hundreds of ships and thousands of seamen were lost before the first of these tugs were delivered.

The Admiralty's main workhorse became the steam driven Saint class tug. This was moderately successful, but many were not delivered until the war was over. After the war, these tugs were sold or leased to commercial operators, who then saw no need to invest in improved tonnage. While the British were using the Saint tugs the Dutch, spurred on by German competition, were developing better tugs and equipment. In 1933 Smit took delivery of the *Zwarte Zee*, the third of that name and the tug of the decade.

In Britain, there was one ray of sunshine. The French Compagnie de Remorquage et de Sauvetage "Les Abeilles" of Le Havre set up a British subsidiary; Overseas Towage & Salvage Co. Ltd (OTS), in 1937. The French company's intention was to continue ordering tugs from UK yards and to transfer them, as second-hand vessels, where possible. Between 1938 and the outbreak of war they took delivery of three tugs, *Neptunia*, *Nereidia* and *Salvonia*. They were only able to transfer the *Nereidia*, which became the *Abeille No 4*. The other two Red Ensign tugs were among those requisitioned by the Navy in 1939. The *Neptunia* was torpedoed 13 September 1939, but the *Abeille No 4* re-joined her remaining sister in June 1940. *Neptunia's* loss is recorded in British Merchant Vessels Lost by Enemy Action, though she is listed as being on charter to, or requisitioned by, the Admiralty.

Not only were these three tugs important in their own right, the Assurance class war buildings were based on the *Salvonia* and the Envoy class on the *Neptunia*. Before the war, OTS and the ship builders Henry Robb had designed a large diesel tug to compete with the *Zwarte Zee*. This became the eight ship Bustler class of 4,200 IHP (3040 BHP) with a 30 ton bollard pull. These fine vessels became the mainstays of the Admiralty deep-sea rescue fleet.

Those in authority knew that the enemy would again try to starve Britain into submission, as they had almost succeeded in doing during the previous conflict. The way the Germans planned to do this was by attacking Britain's merchant fleet, using U-boats supplemented by surface craft and aircraft.

When war was declared the Admiralty requisitioned every tug that could be used for rescue work and many more as harbour tugs. The first rescue tugs were the: *Al Hathera, Coringa, Danube III, Danube V, Danube VI, Englishman, Fairplay Two, Hendon, Kenia, Lady Brassey* (and *Lady Duncannon?), Muria, Neptunia, Nguvu, St Olaves, Salvonia, Saucy, Seaman, Stalwart, Superman* and *Watermeyer*. This last tug was from South Africa and the first from east Africa. In addition, the smaller *Guardsman* and seven of the Thames based Sun tugs were among those taken up as harbour and coastal tugs.

The ships were mostly manned by their peacetime crews, serving under naval discipline under the T124 system: where they had their own subsection T124T. The officers were commissioned in the Royal Naval Reserve, then a reserve of professional merchant seamen and naval pensioners. Others were recruited from among 'small ship men' from the merchant service and the fishing fleets. Most of the tugs flew the White Ensign of the Royal Navy – though others continued to be part of the Merchant Navy and flew the Red Ensign. The naval organisation became the Deep Sea Rescue Tugs (D.S.R.T.). Retired tug- masters and crews were recalled to train new men as quickly as possible, though many had to learn on the job, many being violently sea-sick at first because of the lively motion of the tugs.

The first base was at Campbeltown in the West of Scotland, tugs from there were tasked with towing North Atlantic casualties back to the UK for repair. Those at Harwich, on the south east coast of England, assisted the coastal convoys. As the war progressed, bases were established over much of the world. Later tugs accompanied the convoys across the Atlantic. They were responsible for saving hundreds of torpedoed and weather damaged ships, and many crew.

The fall of the Low Countries and France in May/June 1940 brought a much needed supplement to the rescue tug fleet: *Abeille No 4, Abeille 22, Amsterdam, Antic, Attentif, Champion, Cherbourgoise No 3, Cherbourgoise No 4, Danube, Donau*, Ebro*, Goliath, Hudson*, Lauwerzee*, Indira, Mastodonte, Roode Zee*,Seine*, Schelde*,Thames*, Witte Zee** and *Zwarte Zee** joining. The ten Smit tugs are marked*.

Five Smit tugs were already outside the Netherlands in May 1940, they were: *Thames, Roode Zee, Seine, Hudson* and *Donau*. The first four were on Admiralty service; the *Roode Zee* was lost with all hands when she was torpedoed in April 1944. Others that escaped were *Zwarte Zee , Witte Zee, Schelde, Ebro* and *Lauwerzee*; the first three of these were in Admiralty service, and the last was lost in 1940.
From David Asprey; his source: Colledge - Ships of the Royal Navy.

The history 'Smit 150' states that there were 12, but this does not appear to be correct. A similar number remained in the Netherlands.

Cherbourgoise No 4.   TugTalk.com, photographer unknown

There is also some confusion about the *Witte Zee*. The 1914 built steam tug *Witte Zee* escaped to the UK; but was wrecked off Porth Eymon Point, in Wales, on 12 November 1940. The tug had been on passage from Penzance to Lamlash. Another *Witte Zee* was built in occupied Holland and delivered in 1944; this tug was also wrecked on the UK coast, this time off the Isle of Wight in 1964.

Another early loss was the *Lauwerzee*. On 3 October 1940 she left Falmouth under the command of G. Weltevreden, with the small cable ship *Lady of the Isles* in tow. They sailed with two other cable vessels and a Navy trawler, as escort. An hour after sailing a heavy explosion was heard and Arie Visser, who was on watch on the *Lauwerzee*, saw *Lady of the Isles* break up and sink. One of the other cable vessels picked up three survivors, but three naval reservists were lost; including a Ty. Lieutenant RNVR, her captain? The *Lauwerzee* was then ordered to return to Falmouth with the Navy trawler. At 1530 there was a heavy explosion in the forepart of the tug; the funnel and foremast collapsed and the vessel started to list, and sink, 13 crew members were lost. The only survivor was Arie Visser, who made the loss report. Neither the *Witte Zee* nor the *Lauwerzee* are recorded as Admiralty losses.

From various other sources came the *Caroline Moller, Revue, Sabine, St Dominic, Salvage King* and *Sea Giant,* plus several smaller tugs. This influx coincided with the delivery of the new building *Assurance* and several others of this class. Further Assurance class tugs were delivered until late 1943. With the delivery of *Sesame* in October 1943, 21 had been built, though several had already been lost. The *Sesame* herself was lost during the D-Day landings.

The *Zwarte Zee* was the deep sea rescue tug against which all subsequent designs would be measured. With twin 1,200 brake horsepower diesel engines, geared to a single shaft, the vessel had a free running speed in excess of 15 knots. The tug had a bollard pull of 24 tons and an endurance of 20,000 miles. Horse power was to be a contentious issue. Smit took to quoting IHP, in this case 4,000. They said this meant Indicated Horse Power, a unit normally used for the output of a steam engine.

The U S Navy used the *Zwarte Zee* specification for their 49 ship V4-M-A1 class, with a BHP of 2,320 and a bollard pull of 24 tons. It was not until January 1943, that the first of these tugs were delivered. By the end of June of that year the US Navy had 12. Ten saw service at the Normandy landings, managed by Moran Towing. The arrival of the *Bustler* in May 1942 set a whole new standard in deep-sea rescue tugs. This vessel was a quarter more powerful than the *Zwarte Zee* - with a bollard pull of 30 tons.

BUSTLER class

Built by Henry Robb, based on a design they had prepared for
Overseas Towage and Salvage. Dimensions in feet: 190 (205 o a) x 38.6
x 19 (13 draft), deadweight of 538, speed of 16 knots, range about
17,000 miles, most websites wrongly quote 1,700. Two British Polar 8
cylinder type M 48 M, each 1520 b.h.p., bollard pull at a continuous
rating 30 tons.

Name	Yard No	Pennant	Launched	Notes
BUSTLER	321	W72	4.12.41	1100 g.r.t
GROWLER	328	W105	10.9.42	1100 g.r.t
HESPERIA	329	W106	10.11.42	1100 g.r.t, ex Hesper
MEDIATOR	335	W125	21.6.44	1100 g.r.t
REWARD	336	W164	13.10.44	1136 g.r.t
SAMSONIA	322	W23	1.4.42	1100 g.r.t ex Samson
TURMOIL	337	W169	14.7.44	1136 g.r.t
WARDEN	338	W170	28.6.45	1136 g.r.t

US V4-M-A1 tugs at Normandy – total class size 49.

1,117 g.r.t, 251 n.r.t, 1613 Displacement, 625 Deadweight, speed 14
knots, range 19,000 miles, fuel capacity 538 tons.

Name	Yard	Hull No	Delivered
MOOSE PEAK	General SB	405	Aug 1943
GAY HEAD	General SB	407	Dec 1943
BODIE ISLAND	General SB	408	Dec 1943
GREAT ISAAC	General SB	409	Apr 1944
SABINE PASS	Avondale	40	Apr 1943

SANKATY HEAD	Froemming Bros	5	Jul 1943
FARALLON	Globe SB	101	Jun 1943
TRINIDAD HEAD	Globe SB	103	Jul 1943
BLACK ROCK	Globe SB	109	Nov 1943
HILLSBORO INLET	Pennsylvania SY	280	Sep 1943

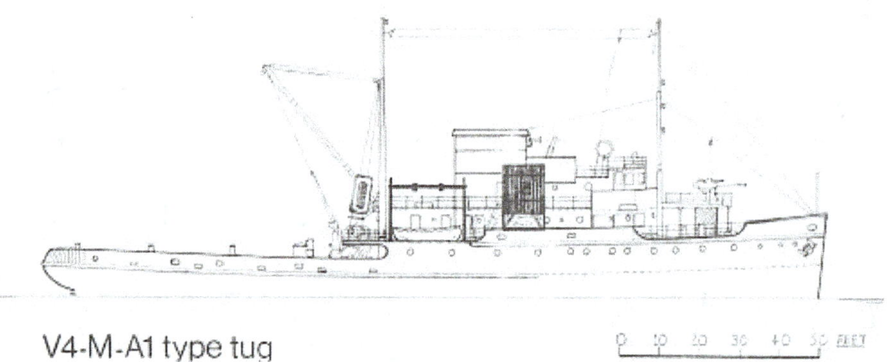

V4-M-A1 type tug

V4-M-A1   **Courtesy Hans van der Ster**

Ministry of War Transport (MOWT) Tugs

The Ministry of War Transport (MOWT), also built a fleet of tugs for operation under the Red Ensign; these were commercially managed. In all there were 120 sea-going/ocean-going tugs and nearly 200 river tugs. Many of the latter group were the war built prefabricated TID tugs, said to be an abbreviation of **Tug, Inshore & Dock**. In accordance with usual MOWT practice, the sea-going/ocean-going tugs, were managed by civilian firms. The TIDs went far and wide, many as deck cargo on merchant ships; they were both naval and civilian manned. Fourteen were at Normandy with army crews.

Managers

J D McLaren & Co Ltd, London

A ship broking firm founded by Jack McLaren MC, a member of the Baltic Exchange. The company had been L Smit & Cos general agents for England and Wales since the 1920s. The Smit tugs that escaped from the Netherlands in May/June 1940 were first put under the management of the Nederlandse Scheepvaart & Handelscommissie, London, but were soon transferred to McLarens. Smit authorised McLaren to negotiate charter arrangements with the U K government. Like the other rescue tugs, the Smit vessels were controlled by the Admiralty, but McLarens kept responsibility for crew wages and the ships remained under the Dutch flag. The tug *Dexterous* was chartered to Smit, to replace a war loss. In addition, McLarens seem to have some involvement in ship management. In 1944 they were managing the *Empire Moonrise* for the Ministry of War Transport and probably other cargo vessels.

In 1944 Jack McLaren and others set up a ship broking company in Colombo. They continued as Smit's agent for a long period after the war. When Smit acquired Overseas Towage and Salvage, McLaren also managed that company from their offices in 24 St Mary Axe. For a few years, they continued to manage dry cargo vessels.

Moran Towing, New York

Incorporated in 1905 this famous U S company can trace its origins back to 1855 when Michael Moran, a 22 year-old Irish immigrant, bought a barge for use on the Eire canal. By 1880 Moran Towing were established as tugboat owners in New York.

In 1905 the company set a record for long distance tows when one of their tugs towed a barge from New York to San Francisco, via Cape Horn, a distance of 13,220 miles.

Eugene Moran Sr. was commissioned in U S Naval Reserve in 1917, his job being to provide the European allies with additional tugs and other craft. In the mid-1930s Moran began replacing their steam tugs with diesels. By 1940 they had a fleet of eleven diesel tugs; one of these was designed to make trans-Atlantic crossings. In 1941 Edmond Moran joined the U.S. Naval Reserve and Eugene Senior came out of retirement to take his place.

During the Allied invasion of Normandy, Edmond managed an armada of tugs and barges that spent ten days ferrying concrete caissons and steel piers across the English Channel to establish man-made harbours. For his role in the D-Day invasion Edmond was promoted to Rear Admiral and awarded the Legion of Merit by the United States and the Croix de Guerre by the French government. He was also named an Honorary Commander (Military Division), of the

Order of the British Empire. He resumed the presidency of Moran Towing in 1946.

During the war Moran Towing had operated 112 tugs, including the ten 195-foot V-4 tugs built by the U.S. government. The company completed 1,153 assignments for the military, losing two tugs and sinking a German submarine off the coast of Florida. (www.fundinguniverse.com/company-histories/Moran-Towing-Corporation.)

Overseas Towage and Salvage, London

The French Compagnie de Remorquage et de Sauvetage "Les Abeilles" of Le Havre had built its tugs in Britain for many years. In the mid-1930s, the French government refused to issue further import licences to the company, who therefore decided to set up a British subsidiary. Overseas Towage & Salvage Co. Ltd was formed in 1937, with offices in London's Kingsway.

The first tugs were managed by the coastal tanker owners C. Rowbotham and later by a member of the Andrews family, who may have been related by marriage to the Rowbothams.

Their Admiralty fleet has been covered in the main text, as has their contribution to the design of various Admiralty Deep Sea Rescue Tugs. In addition, they managed many 'Empire' tugs on behalf of the Ministry of War Transport. By the end of the war, they controlled 26 of these vessels and managed a further five of the parent company's tugs.

In 1959 the company was acquired by L Smit & Co., who closed them down in 1964. Les Abeilles still operates the French Emergency Salvage Tugs, as part of Groupe Bourbon.

Ship Towage (London) Ltd

Formed after the First World War by the amalgamation of William Watkins and the Elliot Steam Tug Co, they then acquired Gamecock Tugs Ltd. William Watkins was the oldest private tug owner in the world, being formed in 1833. Their first tug being the *Monarch,* which appears in Turner's 1839 painting -The Fighting Temeraire.

 By 1939 the company operated 17 steam tugs, including a number suitable for coastal towage work. Five were requisitioned by the Admiralty, two as rescue tugs and the others for harbour work. The company was more involved with the MOWT.

Sun Tugs, London

William Henry James Alexander was born in Milton, Gravesend in 1858. W.H.J. Alexander Ltd began operating from Wapping as a lighterage company in 1883. 1899 saw the beginning of the use of the prefix 'Sun' on all their vessels. WHJ died in 1929 and the business was inherited by his six sons, all tug masters, and two daughters. Besides owning tugs and lighters, the family also owned sailing vessels. William's sons, George and Charles, ran the business after their father's death; they also commanded tugs at Dunkirk. In 1938 they contributed four tugs and 150 barges to the Silvertown Services consortium (part of Tate and Lyle). Thereafter they concentrated on ship towing. (www.thamestugs.co.uk.)

United Towing Co Ltd, Hull

In the 19th Century there were a number of small tug companies operating on the Humber; on 1 January 1914 they agreed to form an association. This led to the incorporation of United Towing in 1921; the new group operated 39 tugs.

By 1926 there were 24 tugs in the fleet; including two new buildings of 226 g.r.t. and one of 369 g.r.t. These three were suitable for sea towing and, by the outbreak of the war, the company had gained expertise in long-distance towing. The following tugs were requisitioned by the Admiralty: *Englishman*, 1939, 487 g.r.t.; *Krooman* 1938, 230 g.r.t.; *Seaman*, 1924, 369 g.r.t. and *Superman*, 1933, 359 g.r.t.

The Salvage Vessels

A similar hasty requisitioning of salvage vessels took place. These were required to deal with those casualties that were beyond the first aid help that the tugs could provide. At the outbreak of the First World War, the Admiralty had neither salvage vessels, nor a department to run them. Commercial salvage was fragmented, the largest salvage organisations were those operated by the big ports such as London and Liverpool; while the smaller ports relied on local commercial salvors. A number of ship owners also operated salvage craft and there were specialist organisations; many could trace their history back to the 19th century. Seeing the need, the Admiralty acquired such vessels as were available and converted a number of small warships for the work.

 Civilian managers, such as the Liverpool Salvage Association (LSA), provided the management and expertise. The Liverpool Salvage Association was formed in 1857 by local ship owners, underwriters, and merchants. The Glasgow Salvage Association was formed in the same year. From the start both were intended to be non-profit making organisations.

Under its General Manager, Frank Lowe, and Chief Salvage Officer Frederick Young, the Liverpool Salvage Association, supervised much of the Admiralty Salvage in the First World War. So successful were they that Captain Young was knighted and made a Commodore in the Royal Naval Reserve. Sir Fredrick Young became a legend in the industry and beyond. In 1924 the two organisations merged to become the Liverpool and Glasgow Salvage Association, with offices in both cities.

At the outbreak of the Second World War, there were those in the Admiralty who believed that LGSA would again lead the salvage effort, but their manager, G R Critchley, and chief salvage officer, Captain Kay, would only agree to take responsibility for the West Coast of the UK. They eventually managed four ships for the Admiralty. They remain in business as surveyors.

There was also a London Salvage Association; they did not operate ships but sent surveyors all over the world to look after underwriters interests.

Most of the vessels were old at the beginning of the First World War and at the end, they were disposed of. The longest-lived of the salvage vessels was LSA's *Ranger*, which had been built in 1880 as a steam gunboat, she continued in service until the 1950s. Only a few dumb (non-propelled) lifting craft were retained after the war and most of these went in the 1930s. Much of the expertise was also lost; fortunately some skilled people went back to the commercial companies.

As a new conflict became more likely, the Nation again found itself without a unified salvage organisation. Britain was short of just about everything, so the absence of a salvage capability probably did not seem of great importance. That was until it was realised how easily aircraft bombing, mining, or torpedoing ships could block the ports. The Admiralty set up a committee to report on how a salvage organisation could be resurrected; Admiral Dewar was put in charge. The committee suggested that the quickest way was to requisition all suitable ships and to hand them over to civilian managers, who were often the owners of the ships in the first place. This is what happened soon after the war began.

Because of their stalwart work in the First World War, the Liverpool and Glasgow Salvage Association, as they had become, were to look after the whole of the West Coast from Cape Wrath to Land's End. Metal Industries, who had taken over the famous Scapa firm of Cox & Danks, were to cover the East Coast from Cape Wrath to Harwich – including the Northern Isles. The Port of London Authority (PLA), handled Harwich to North Foreland. From here to Land's End was left to Commander (later Captain), Doust to 'coordinate'. The East Coast section was later sub divided to include Leith Towage and Salvage and T Rounds of Scarborough.

Doust and his team then approached Dover Harbour Board (DHB), who had for many years operated their own sea going tugs; DHB agreed to take responsibility for the coast from North Foreland to Beachy Head. Now the problem was what to do about the rest of the English Channel. By the summer of 1940, there was no cover for the South Coast and many of the requisitioned ships were still without managers. Doust knew of the Southampton salvor Risdon Archibald Beazley (RAB) from his involvement with the salvage operation on the *English Trader* in 1938.

The Doust team were surprised by what they found when they went to Southampton. Here was an operator with a fleet of ships, albeit some of them rather small; and an impressive store of salvage equipment – mostly ex-Admiralty stock from the earlier war. RAB, never the man to overlook an opportunity, had over the preceding three years, bought up just about every ship that had, or could have, a salvage capability. He was young and he had assembled a keen young team around him. Their base at Bitterne fronted onto the River Itchen and extended from there to the trunk road that joined Portsmouth and

Southampton. Bitterne had a railway station on the line from Southampton Central and Docks to Portsmouth. There was also a local airport (the home of the Spitfire fighter plane). During the visit, it was agreed that Mr S W Giddings, the Company Secretary of Risdon Beazley Ltd (RB), would provide a list of the ships that they operated and the equipment would be listed for the Admiralty.

Then the conversation turned to the surplus ships. We only have Doust's account of this part of the conversation, though it agrees with the tale that was handed down in later years. It was said to have gone, 'well Mr Beazley we have more ships on our hands than we would like', RAB – 'how many do you have', 'well with your vessels we will have over thirty', RAB 'we'll take them'. Doust adds that Beazley also said, 'as far as I am concerned the sky is the limit': the phrase does not sound like one of RAB's, but the willingness to accept a challenge does.

When Giddings' letter arrived in London, it listed a total of 19 ships, including even the Southampton 'sludge' vessel *Bargate*. Times were difficult, but the Admiralty decided that they were not so desperate that they needed a sludge boat. The Ministry of War Transport also questioned whether RB's coaster *Palmston* would not be more useful as a cargo carrier. As it was, only the *Bargate*, the *Poole Dredger No 2*, the *Topmast No 3* and the tug *Aid* are not listed in the 1945 fleet. The *Aid* had been taken up but was lost in 1940.

The additional ships that came under RB's management from 1 August 1940 were as varied as the fleet that they had contributed. They included the *Lady Southborough, Forde,* and the *Gallions Reach* ; all had been at Dunkirk. The other vessels were: *Dapper, Doria, Dormouse, Foremost 18, Freija, Longtow, Maggie Lough, Nessus, Ramier, Richard* (later renamed *Richard II*), *Roselyne*, *Thoma II*, *Trottebec*, *Venture III*, *Watercock* and *Wayfarer*.

Beazley's area of responsibility was to be from Beachy Head to Land's End. Right from the start the boundaries seem to have been somewhat fluid; three of the RB managed vessels were based at Harwich and journeyed even further afield. At least one went as far as Scapa Flow. The Harwich three were: *Freija*, *Foremost 18* and *Forde*. The latter had been the first cross channel car ferry: between them, they worked along the east coast.

Metal Industries, who supplied three salvage officers and two ships, eventually settled for a 'compensation' payment of £7,000. It is a measure of the responsibility that Risdon Beazley shouldered that they were awarded £20,000.

For Operation Neptune, and the subsequent salvage work throughout north-west Europe, Metal Industries provided the McKenzie brothers, as Principal Salvage Officer and deputy. Risdon Beazley became the project managers, taking over the day-to-day management of all the salvage vessels to the period of the landings. The husbandry remained with the ship mangers.

War Built Salvage Ships

By 1943 new salvage vessels were being delivered, those for the British were divided into three classes:

The British built King Salvor class, 200 feet in length, 1,500 HP steamers, were designed for salvage work in distant waters. They were equipped with workshops, diving gear, welding and cutting tools. They were not, however, designed as lifting craft and this shortcoming meant that they seem not to have been popular with the salvage officers. Six were put under Risdon Beazley's management, but none were at Normandy.

The American equivalents of the King Salvor class were the BARS ships. One American source says that these vessels were built to a British design and specification, but it has not been possible to confirm this. These wooden vessels were 183 feet in length and were propelled by diesel electric engines of 1,200 BHP. A number were built for operation by US forces. Four were put under RB management; most of the delivery crews were British seamen from the Montreal and New York seamen's pool.

The first, the *American Salvor* arrived in the UK in November 1943, with convoy SC146. Captain G L Wallwork assumed command on the 1st December. The First Mate, R W Lennard, later took command of the *Help* for the landings; he was awarded an OBE for his services in France. The *Lincoln Salvor* arrived in January 1944 with convoy SC 152. Six of her crew had deserted in the USA; they seem to have been 'big ship men' who must have been horrified at the thought of crossing the Western Ocean in mid-winter in so small a vessel. Captain Griffith took command and later the Mate, Mr Walker, was promoted Master. The *Boston Salvor*, Captain Eidick, a Latvian, and the *Southampton Salvor* did not arrive until the end of March 1944 with convoy SC155, which included 25 LSTs (Landing Ship – Tank). All four were part of the salvage fleet for the landings, as were their US flagged sisters: USS *Swivel, Diver,* and *Brant*.

The remaining self-propelled class of salvage vessel was the Coastal Class. The design was conceived early in 1942 to meet the need for wreck dispersal vessels. The Admiralty Director of Salvage realised that the design would also be useful for salvage work. The Admiralty decided that port clearance would be a priority and ordered nine of the Coastal Class for the Salvage Department, rather than for the Director of Wreck Dispersal.

The outline design was passed to Smith's Dock, who handled the detailed work. In the mid-thirties Smith's had designed an improved type of whale catcher. They developed this design to become the workhorse of the North Atlantic escort fleet, the 'Flower'-class corvette, 277 of these were built in the UK and Canada. Smith's did a similarly good job on the Coastals. They were given the order to build all of the class, but the last four were later transferred to other yards. These handy ships were 179 feet overall, 150' BP, with a 35.5′ beam. They could lift 100 tons over the bow or up to 250 ton as a 'belly lift'.

A Coastal Class on trials (*Lifeline?*). Risdon Beazley photograph.

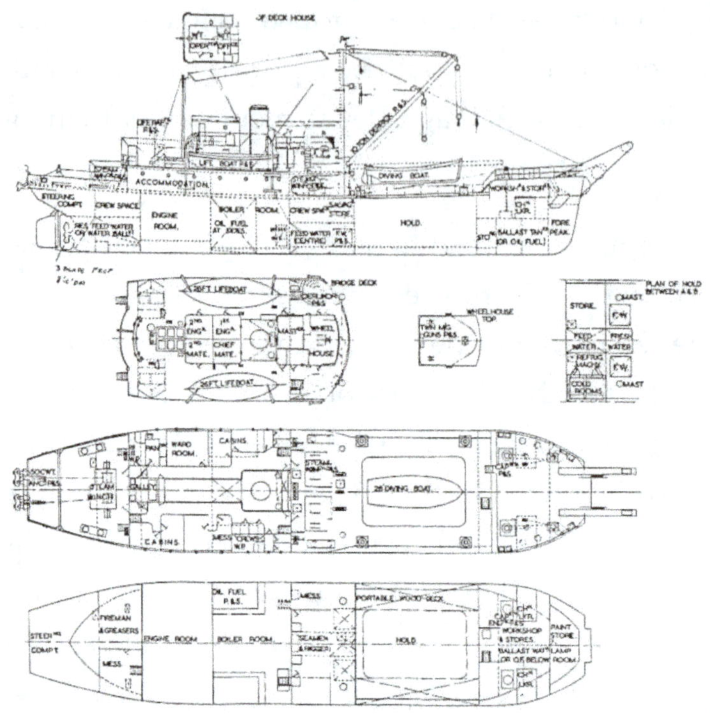

Plan of the Coastal class, as built.   Courtesy David Sowdon

Smith's completed the *Dispenser* in October 1943. After trials, she was handed over to Risdon Beazley. Captain Frank Hunter took her to the Mediterranean, beginning work in Naples at the end of November. The next four were available for Normandy. They were designed to be used in pairs, but were not used in that way in France. Instead ,each was teamed up with one of the older requisitioned lifting vessels.

Additionally, dumb (non-propelled), Admiralty Lifting Craft were built. These also operated in pairs and were capable of lifting eight hundred tons, or one thousand tons as a pair. ALCs 1-6 had been built back in 1897 and LC 7 in 1912. LC 8-11 were built on the Clyde in 1940. Twenty 'Camels' provided further lifting capacity.

The Crews

Until after the Great War the service had been known as the Mercantile Marine. Later it was renamed the British Merchant Navy, with the Sovereign becoming Master of the Merchant Navy and the Fishing Fleets. In 1919 a standard uniform was authorized. It never was a navy, but the title was probably selected because of a problem that had occurred during the First World War. Captain Charles Fryatt, Master of the Railway Packet *Brussels*, had attempted to ram U-boats. When the Germans finally captured him ,they held that, as he was a civilian, he was guilty of being a franc-tireur. He was sentenced to death and executed the same evening. In 1919 his body was exhumed and brought back to England. After a memorial service he was reburied at Dovercourt, Harwich.

During the depression seamen who had jobs hung onto them, while others trudged around the shipping offices looking for work. Master Mariners signed on as Able Seamen and Quartermasters, and many left the industry altogether.

Both the quality of the merchant ships, and the conditions of employment, varied widely. At best ,seamen were given continuous employment, decent accommodation and food. At the worst, living conditions were disgusting and food was inadequate. Until 1941 wages were stopped as soon as a ship was sunk. For the unfortunate men on the tramp ships conditions never really improved.

In addition to its peacetime role, which became essential for the Nation's survival, the merchant fleet would be needed to move war materiel and troops and to support evacuations and invasions. At the outbreak of the Second World War, the total strength of the British

Merchant Navy was only 157,000. About two thirds of the crews were from mainland Britain and the balance came from the Commonwealth and other countries.

In peacetime, the merchant fleet brought 67 million tons of cargo into the UK annually. This included 22 million tons of food, twenty eight and a half million tons of raw materials and nine and a half million tons of oil fuel. This met more than half of the country's meat requirements, 70% of its cheese and sugar, nearly 80% of fruits, about 90% of cereals and fats, and all of the oil fuel. (These figures are from a Wikipedia article). The ships brought in all the tobacco and tea, and much of the bread flour, that became so important once the war started. It is difficult to underestimate the importance of 'a cup of char, a sarnie and a fag' to the beleaguered people. One of the principal strategies of the Axis was to attack shipping bound for the UK, restricting British industry and with the intention of starving the nation into submission. To deal with the extreme shortages the Ministry of Food imposed rationing.

Before the Tudors fighting fleets were made up of requisitioned merchant ships; still manned by their peacetime crews, but carrying soldiers. The Master remained in command of the ship and he and the Mates sailed it to meet the requirements of the Captain, an Army officer. This rather peculiar arrangement continued even when the Tudor Kings and Queens had dedicated ships built. Masters, and Masters Mates, remained in the Royal Navy until Victorian times.

The previous major maritime invasion of France was the Battle of Sluys, six hundred years before. Then a fleet of 250 or more British trading ships, carrying longbow men, overcame the French and their Genoese allies.

The Australian and New Zealanders remember the Mercantile Marine's contribution in another landing, this time in the First World War. The merchant ships took our troops and in many cases landed them in the ships' lifeboats. The merchant seamen also came under the deadly fire from the Turkish guns.

It is also interesting to note that the great majority of wounded in that campaign were taken in the ships' lifeboats, with merchant seamen manning the oars, to the hospital ships which were waiting offshore. The merchant ships evacuated most of our troops from Gallipoli to Alexandria, Lemnos and Cyprus and then transported the wounded home. *The above text is courtesy of the Royal Australian Navy History Unit and the Australian War Memorial; with minor additions.*

Blue Funnel Apprentices say that they earned to right to be called Midshipmen to acknowledge their contribution to the landings; but they were by no means the only Apprentices who manned the boats. Nor were the ANZACs the only troops to be landed; many British and French soldiers were put ashore and many are buried there.

It was therefore appropriate that the merchant ships were to play an important part in these new landings as they had done in 1943 in the Mediterranean.

The Royal Navy tended to look down on the merchant service and even the other fighting services. In the case of the merchantmen, this could be because so few of their officers were from Public Schools, and many had worked their way up 'from the deck'. The popular saying at sea was the naval officers were gentlemen, trying to be sailors; merchant officers were sailors, trying to be gentlemen; and the RNVR were neither, trying to be both.

By 1939 a foreign-going ship carried a minimum of three Mates (also known as Chief, Second and Third Officers); six or more Engineers, four on a steamer; a Deck Department of eight under a Boatswain and a Carpenter and another eight ratings in the Engine Room, under a Donkeyman: there was a similar sized Catering Department and a single Radio Officer. Between two and four Apprentices or Cadets were usually carried. During the war most carried three Radio Officers.

Defence was provided by between two and eighteen gunners, depending on the size of the ship; these came from the Royal Artillery and/or the Royal Navy. On British ships the DEMS gunners were signed on as 'sailors' or 'deck hands' and were under command of the Master, one of the Mates, usually the Second Officer, being the Gunnery Officer. On US ships, the Armed Guard were separate from the ship's manning and were under the charge of their own officer.

For the landings, the merchant ships were provided with two Seaborne Observers from the Royal Observer Corps. These 796 men were all volunteers; they stood 'watch and watch', four hours on and four hours off - a tiring routine. They were civilians but were given the rank of Petty Officer RN for the duration.

Two Seaborne Observers lost their lives and several were injured during the landings: but 22 survived their ships being sunk.

In a signal Wing Commander P.B. Lucas, air staff officer, said:

> The general impression amongst the Spitfire wings, covering our land and naval forces over and off the beach-head, appears to be that in the majority of cases the fire has come from warships and not from the

merchant ships. Indeed I personally have yet to hear a single pilot report that a merchant vessel had opened fire on him"

Air Chief Marshal Trafford Leigh-Mallory confirmed this in an appreciation sent to all ROC personnel.

Uniform was only worn by the officers on foreign-going ships. Petty officers and ratings usually wore dungaree trousers and shirts, with an old jacket in colder weather. They wore a wide variety of headgear from flat caps to hand-made nautical caps. Few on coastal cargo ships wore any kind of uniform. Earlier in the century, some coastal masters had worn a bowler hat.

Ships leaving the United Kingdom signed on a crew at their departure port. With the exception of the Master, the Mate and Chief Engineer and the Apprentices, the crew of a tramp would have been sourced in this way. In Merchant Navy slang, they were known as a 'crowd', as in, 'she had a Glasgow crowd.' The ships of the better companies were manned mostly, or even entirely, by 'company men.' Either way they usually signed Articles of Agreement which called for them to serve for a period of two years, or until they next returned to the UK. The 'Articles' set out their working conditions and the minimum amount of food they were to receive each month, known as 'the Board of Trade whack.' It also limited their area of operation to between 72° north and 60° south. Coasters and ships that called at the UK frequently signed six monthly running agreements, rather than signing off each time they reached the UK.

Ratings and petty officers were paid overtime for hours worked in excess of 64 hours a week, though there were exceptions for days of arrival and sailing. Officers, engineers, and apprentices were not usually paid overtime; this often resulted in the apprentices working considerably longer than the basic week. Time spent on boat and fire drills, or cleaning accommodation, did not count towards the hours. Officers had to buy uniforms for tropical, temperate and Arctic service and the deck officers also bought their own sextants.

For some months prior to the invasion merchant seamen signing on or off ships were asked if they would be willing to sign' V' Articles. Those who enquired were told that the 'V' indicated that they were prepared to volunteer for the Mass Invasion of Europe and that they would be required to work on any ship, or ashore. The others were just told that it would entitle them to an additional weekly ration of 200 cigarettes - valuable currency then.

The National Archives files in BT391 list just over 32,000 men and at least one woman. Second Engineer Officer Victoria Alexandrina (or Alexandria), Drummond was a goddaughter of Queen Victoria. She had taken part in the evacuation of the south of France, as the Second Engineer on the *Har Zion*.

Miss Drummond was awarded the MBE and the Lloyd's War Medal for Bravery at Sea for single-handedly remaining at the controls of the Panamanian flagged cargo ship *Bonita* during an attack by a German bomber. After volunteering, she was sent to the British tanker *Karabagh,* as Fourth Engineer. There is no record of this ship taking part in Operation Neptune, but the Final Assembly plan of the Solent anchorage shows a water tanker *Karabach* in Anchorage 25. Miss Drummond had been repeatedly prevented from serving in the British Merchant Navy during the war. She seems to have been frustrated again, as the tanker appears to have been kept at Spithead supplying water to the ships of the invasion fleet.

Other equally intrepid women were the US war correspondent
Martha Gellhorn and the British reporter Iris Carpenter. Gellhorn's
obituary said 'without official press credentials she reached the
beaches of Normandy after hiding in the lavatory of a hospital ship.'
Somehow or other Iris Carpenter, a British woman who had been a
war reporter for the *Daily Herald,* managed to wangle her way onto a
Tank Landing Craft that was repatriating casualties.

More than 90% of the seamen volunteered and were accepted, but
there are no figures to indicate how many did so purely for the
cigarettes! Others were rejected because of their age. As explained in
the Tugs chapter, many of the salvage and tug crew were already
engaged, as T124T or T124X and appear in BT 390 with other T124
agreements. Other agreements of this type include: F124, T125, T777
and the RASC.

Young officers who qualified for their certificates early in 1944 were
told that they might be required to command landing craft; again the
numbers who did, if any, have not been recorded. Some young MN
officers have unexplained gaps in their service records about this
time. Certain other operations were put on hold for the duration of
the landings.

Working Up

Each of the five Assault Forces were identified with a code letter; which we can now see corresponded to the name of their landing beaches. Working from west to east, they were:

Force U made up of US troops, with a small unit of British commandos. In addition to a large fleet of LST and other landing craft their ships were: *Barnett*, *Bayfield* (HQ Ship), *Bienville* (Troopship), *Empire Gauntlet* (LSI(L)), *Excelsior* (Troopship), *Explorer* (Troopship) and *Joseph T Dickman* (Troopship). With the exception of the *Empire Gauntlet*, the ships are American. They were mainly based in Devon. Their exercises will always be remembered for the disaster of Operation Tiger.

Force O were based in the Dorset ports of Weymouth, Portland and, possibly, Poole. Their ships were: *Achernar* (US), *Amsterdam*, *Anne Arundel* (US), *Ben-my-Chree*, *Borinquen* (US Troopship), *Charles Carroll* (US), *Dorothea L Dix* (US), *Empire Anvil*, *Empire Javelin*, *Exchequer* (US Troopship), *George S Simonds* (US Troopship), *George W Goethals* (US Troopship), *Henrico* (US), HMS *Invicta*, *Marine Raven* (US Troopship), HMS *Prince Baudouin*, HMS *Prince Charles*, HMS *Prince Leopold*, *Princess Maud*, *Samuel Chase* (US), *Susan B Anthony* (US Troopship), *Thomas Jefferson* (US), *Thurston* (US). Those with no nationality shown are British.

The families of two young RNVR officers have recorded their experiences online. By a coincidence, they were both on the *Empire Javelin*. One was in charge of the DEMS gunners, which he says were eighteen strong, and the other was the Divisional Officer in charge of LCA Assault Flotilla 551. The Gunnery Officer seemed to think that he was second in command of the ship, but that is the function of the MN Chief Officer. Perhaps he was confused by the fact that he reported to the Master, as any Head of Department would do. A Lieutenant RN was the Senior Naval Officer Transport and therefore the senior naval officer on board.

The Divisional Officer was already stationed in Plymouth when the newly built *Empire Javelin* arrived from the United States in February 1944. A few days were spent sorting out operational procedures before the ship sailed to the Holy Loch in Scotland. There they came under the orders of a Commodore in the US Navy. While training in Scotland they encountered worse weather than their colleagues in the south; though they may have cursed it at the time, it stood them in good stead when bad conditions were encountered at Normandy.

The Force G ships, from Southampton and the Solent, were the British ships: *Cameronia* (Troopship), *City of Canterbury* (Troopship), *Empire Arquebus, Empire Crossbow, Empire Halberd, Empire Lance, Empire Mace, Empire Rapier, Empire Spearhead,* HMS *Glenroy, Leopoldville* (Belgian Troopship), *Louth* (Troopship), *Neuralia* (Troopship) , *Pampas* (delayed), *Victoria.*

This Force was not formed until 1 March 1944, which put it at a considerable disadvantage. It was tasked with transporting and landing the 50th (Northumberland) Division. In the six weeks from Mid-March four Brigade exercises were carried out in the Studland area. The Force was transferred from Dorset to the Southampton - Solent area on 28 April.

The J Force ships, which were already based in Southampton and the Solent, were: *Biarritz* (reserve), HMS *Brigadier, Canterbury, Cheshire*

(Troopship), *Clan Lamont, Devonshire* (Troopship), *Duke of Argyll*, HMS *Duke of Wellington, Isle of Guernsey, Isle of Thanet* (also reserve HQ ship), *Lady of Mann, Lairds Isle, Lancashire* (Troopship), *Llangibby Castle, Longford* (Troopship), *Mecklenburg* (Dutch), *Monowai* (New Zealand), HMCS *Prince David* (Canadian), HMCS *Prince Henry* (Canadian), HMS *Queen Emma, St Helier, Ulster Monarch, Worcestershire* (Troopship).

This force started its training much earlier than the others. It had grown from a team set up in October 1942, under Captain Hughes-Hallett, which had taken part in the landing in Sicily. As Force J, it began training in September 1943, with the 3rd Canadian Division. Through the winter they completed twelve assault exercises, plus ferry and beach reconnaissance.

The S Force was to sail from ports between Portsmouth and Shoreham. The ships were: HMS *Glenearn*, HMS *Largs* (HQ ship), *Empire Battleaxe, Empire Broadsword, Empire Cutlass, Maid of Orleans, Princess Margaret*, HMS *Prins Albert*.

Under the command of Rear-Admiral A.G. Talbot, this force trained in Scotland, with its Headquarters at Inverness. Training with the 3rd British Infantry Division started in December. They were restricted in their assault training area, and it was not until late March that they were able practice the assault together.

As outlined in the report about the *Empire Javelin*, the stormy Scottish weather caused great difficulties and the loss of some personnel and craft. The experience gained in these conditions stood them in good stead. In April 1944, the force moved south to its Portsmouth Assembly Area.

The reader will notice that the number a ships allocated to each force varies considerably; presumably, some had more LSTs than others.

Later exercises took place on the south coast; though the LSIs were closely involved, the detail of these operations is not really part of the Merchant Navy story. However ,in outline:

The first was Exercise Smash, which took place in Studland Bay, Dorset, on 18 April 1944. It is remembered for three things. Live ammunition was used, the DD tanks were shown to have grave shortcomings, and the whole exercise was watched by the top brass.

The Duplex Drive tanks had a canvas skirt that was supposed to enable them to 'swim' ashore. They were the brainchild of a British general who had come out of retirement and were called Percy Hobart's 'funnies'. For Exercise Smash, Valentine tanks were used; several of them sank in choppy seas, drowning six soldiers. This form of modification was still used at Normandy, this time with Sherman tanks. While they successfully got ashore at the British Juno beach, they were a disaster at the American beaches. The official explanation was that the Americans launched them too far offshore; but this was only part of the story.

The exercise was watched, from the safety of a giant pillbox called Fort Henry, by King George VI, Prime Minister Winston Churchill, and the Supreme Allied Commander General Dwight Eisenhower.

On the 26 April, the troops of Force U boarded their transports for Operation Tiger. The landing site was Slapton beach in Devon, which had been chosen because it was similar to Utah beach were the actual landing would take place. Thirty thousand troops had embarked on nine landing American Tank Landing Ships. Again, live ammunition was used and General Eisenhower added a naval bombardment to give reality to the exercise. Unfortunately, there was confusion about the time of landing and the second wave was shelled while approaching the beach. It was rumoured that up to 450 men died.

More disaster followed. A convoy, escorted by a single British Corvette, and carrying combat engineers and their vehicles, was attacked by German E-boats. To add to the confusion the British and the Americans were using different radio frequencies.

Two of the LSTs sank, with the loss of 626 Army and Navy personnel. A third managed to make it to shore, but lost 123 sailors. To add to the confusion a fourth was damaged, again by 'friendly fire.

The final series of exercises were codenamed Fabius, these were:

Fabius 1. The 1st Infantry Division and the 29th Infantry Division (US); again at Slapton Sands.

Fabius 2. The 50th Infantry Division at Hayling Island.

Fabius 3. The 3rd Canadian Infantry Division at Bracklesham Bay.

Fabius 4. The 3rd Infantry Division at Littlehampton.

Fabius exercises 5 and 6 involved British and American troops who would be involved in the build-up. The western follow-up force came from Falmouth and Plymouth and the eastern one from the Thames estuary, between Southend and Felixstowe.

The handful of photographs of the LSIs while under the Red Ensign date from this period. The greater number were taken from August onwards, as the ships were taken over by the Royal Navy.

Routeing

The tides in the English Channel are rather unusual; when it is low water at the western end it is high water at the eastern end and vice versa. This would suggest that there is little or no tidal range at the mid-point, about where the intended crossing point would be. This is not so because shallow water and the shape of the coastlines, especially the Cherbourg peninsular, has a considerable modifying effect on the tides. It causes double tides on the English side, between Portland and Selsey,; with a maximum range of five metres at Southampton, where there is a double high water. On the Normandy side, the tidal range is up to six metres. In the middle of the English Channel, currents can reach three knots at springs; not very significant if you are in a fifteen knot ship, but a problem for a tug with a forward speed of five knots.

In 1944 tides were still calculated using a machine that had been manufactured as far back as 1872, to a design by William Thomson. It had been upgraded in 1942. In 1892, Thomson was raised to the peerage as Baron Kelvin of Largs; he was Britain's first scientific peer and the analysis of tides was only a small part of his work.

Edward Roberts produced an improved version of the original Kelvin machine near the end of the century. Both machines were mechanical analogue computers, which incorporated dozens of brass gears, pulleys and wires. They were housed at the Bidston Observatory of the Liverpool Tidal Institute. There were similar machines in the United States and, probably, elsewhere.

If the harmonic constituents of the tides were known, the machines would produce a tidal curve for any location. The harmonic constituents were deduced from the analysis of observations of tides at a particular site, usually a large (Standard), port. To arrive at reliable figures, and eliminate other features such as meteorological effects, these measurements need to be taken over a period. Le Havre and Cherbourg were the only two Normandy ports for which such records existed. The smaller ports in between are known as Secondary Ports, for these the times of High and Low water are obtained by adding or subtracting a figure from a nearby Standard Port. This requires quite a lot of interpolation. These adjustments had been computed using a very limited number of observations and even these figures did not exist for the landing beaches. It was known that the difference in tide times between Utah beach in the west and Sword beach in the east was an hour and twenty minutes.

To obtain as much data as possible the British made a number of secret visits to the enemy beaches, these became known as 'tip and run' visits. They also took soil samples from the beaches, so that scientists could assess the load bearing capabilities of the sand. All but one team returned safely; but their tide and current measurements were, understandably, limited. In 1943 Commander W I Farquharson RN, the Admiralty superintendent of tides at the Hydrographic Office, approached Dr A T Doodson, the Director of the Liverpool Tidal Institute. He outlined the problem, without disclosing the site.

In peacetime, the Liverpool Tidal Institute calculated worldwide tides for the Admiralty, who published the figures in five volumes of tables. By the time the need for accurate tidal data for the landings was identified, the observatory's total staff had been reduced to Arthur Doodson and six young women; even they had other duties such as fire watching between shifts.

Farquharson took eleven pairs of harmonic constants for a 'Position Z' to Doodson,; with a hand written note on Hydrographic Office paper.

Doodson and his team of ladies, fed the data into the 'big brass machines' and produced the figures for the months of April to July 1944. The deductions made, from the very limited data available, proved to be accurate. Doodson said later that he guessed where Position Z was.

At the Hydrographic Office, the computations were used to provide a diagram for each of the five landing beaches. This diagram showed not only the times of low water and the length of the high water stand, but also the times of moonlight and the Astronomical, Nautical, and Civil twilights from 5 June to the 21 June.

The Germans realised the importance of the Tidal Institute and planned to bomb it. The British traitor William Joyce, or Lord Haw Haw as he was nicknamed, predicted during one of his propaganda broadcasts that 'by morning, Bidston will be no more.' Though hundreds of windows were shattered and many doors destroyed in the ensuing raid, the precious equipment, in two separate basement rooms, was undamaged.

Because all of the beaches were encumbered with booby-trapped obstacles the Allies opted to land at low water, rather than high water as the Germans expected. By doing so, at first light, the tank traps could be seen, even though it meant that the assault troops would have to cross a wide expanse of beach under the German guns. They were to be preceded by clearance teams who were to make safe breaches in the defences.

It is generally recorded that, by landing at the time of full moon, the invaders would be landing at the maximum spring tides; but top o' tide lags the moon by a couple of days.

One of the many problems that the planners had to solve was how to route the ships, some with inexperienced navigators, safely across the Channel. To do so meant keeping to narrow, swept channels and avoiding collisions with other allied shipping. They could do nothing about the other problem of action by the enemy.

Most routes would converge at a rendezvous point about twenty nautical miles south of Portsmouth, again designated 'Z'. This became known to all as Piccadilly Circus. From there they would enter 'The Spout' and then follow one of the two routes to their own beach. These ten channels fanned out from The Spout, each had to be swept for mines first and clearly marked with buoys, a mammoth task. There were two exceptions: Force U would pick up their route at 50° 10' North and Force S would go direct to their channel at 50° 05' North. One question was, how would the minesweepers, and before them the pathfinders, navigate across the featureless English Channel, with its strong currents?

The Channel packets, many of them now to serve as Infantry Landing Ships, used to assess their progress by engine revolutions. This was not as strange as it sounds; even when navigating across the ocean the bridge and the engine room always compared the distance run, one by sights and the other by revolutions. Though the bridge and the engine room were often miles apart- this was known as 'slip'!

The Admiralty turned to a version of the Gee system that the RAF used for bomber navigation. This was not particularly accurate, but it beat what had gone before. The Gee master station was at Bulbarrow Hill, near Blandford, Dorset, with slaves at Truleigh Hill on the Downs behind Shoreham-by-Sea and at West Prawle near Salcombe. The monitor being on the Isle of Purbeck.

A problem was that the Germans were aware of Gee and could probably jam it. Eight hundred and sixty invasion ships were fitted with Gee, which the Navy called Outfit QH. But Gee was not sufficiently accurate for the pathfinders and the minesweepers; for them the Admiralty used the more recently developed Decca Navigator system, which they called QM.

The Decca Navigator was the brainchild of an American engineer and inventor, William J. O'Brien. Bill O'Brien had to take a two-year career break to get treatment for tuberculosis. Not one to waste the time he had to spend in the sanatorium, he came up with the idea of position fixing by comparing the phases of continuous wave transmissions. Experiments were carried out in California, but he could not get the US military to take an interest.

One of O'Brien's friends was Harvey F. Schwarz, an American who worked for the British Decca Record Company, who took over. Decca and Schwartz offered the idea to the Air Ministry; but Sir Robert Watson-Watt, the father of RADAR, rejected it as being prone to jamming and interference. So Decca went ahead with trials of the system at their own expense and solved the various problems that arose. After this the British Admiralty started to take an interest.

In 1942 successful trials were run off Anglesey and in early March 1943 the Admiralty ordered 27 receivers and the transmitter gear from

Decca. The equipment was delivered to the Royal Navy by mid-May and training began; further tests were carried out in January 1944.

The existence of the system was top secret. A master station was erected near Chichester, its western Red slave near Swanage and the eastern Green slave a mile inland from Beachy Head. A decoy transmitter was built on the Isle of Sheppey. Twenty one of the Decca sets were supplied to the mine sweeping fleet, plus one each to the five Assault Headquarters Ships and one each to two Harbour Defence Motor Launches. Each was supplied with charts for the landing areas overlaid with the red and green lines of the Decca lattice. The lattice lines had been computed by another team of ladies, this time at the Admiralty Signals Establishment, where they worked protected by an armed guard. The charts on the HDMLs, and one assumes the other ships, were sealed and were not to be opened until a code message was received.

The system went live early on the 5 June. Bill O'Brien was one of the first civilians to realise that the landings were underway when the prototype receiver that he kept in his London home activated. The Decca Navigator proved to be more accurate than Gee, though it was prone to a problem called lane slipping. It was also subject to what became known as fixed and variable errors.

The midget submarines X20 and X23 were in position by 2359 on 4 June, for a landing on the 5 June. X23 had a navigation specialist on board and their task was to mark the limits of the assault area. They had had an unpleasant crossing in the boisterous weather and were constantly shipping water, which had to be baled using hand pumps. Then, because of the postponement, they spent the nineteen hours of daylight on the 5 June lying submerged close to the enemy coast, with no way of replenishing their air supply.

While fixing their positions later, the officers of both craft were washed off the casing and had to be recovered from the sea. The submarines remained in position throughout the initial assault and then until the Trinity House lightships could take over their positions on 18 June. A number of Harbour Defence Motor Launches were also employed as channel markers. HDML 1383 and HDML 1387 marked channels three and four to Omaha, they were the ones fitted with Decca Navigators.

Other HDMLs went ahead of the main mine sweeping fleet. Starting in the afternoon of the 5 June ten channels were to be swept, two for each beach. The channels were aligned first with the Red Decca lanes and then with the Green lanes. This is probably the reason that there is a dog's leg in the channels

Over 300 minesweepers were involved in the work. They had been deployed on the morning of the 4 June, expecting that the assault would start on the following day. Their minimum sweeping speed was 7.5 knots; below this speed, the sweeps would not stream properly, nor would they cut through the mine moorings.

Like the many other craft, the sweepers received the recall signal, which they were unable to acknowledge because of the need to maintain radio silence. The 14th mine sweeping flotilla was sweeping ahead of a convoy approaching the rendezvous 'Piccadilly Circus' when they had unexpectedly found mines. When the recall message arrived, they had already started clearance work and the commander decided that he should complete the task. Two destroyers saw the sweepers were not responding to the signal and approached the flotilla to contact them by semaphore. In doing so, they entered the area that was still not swept and one became surrounded by floating mines. The destroyers were extricated and a fast American PT despatch boat was sent into Portsmouth to advise the ANCXF. It was decided that the mines had probably been jettisoned by a German craft, rather than being part of a minefield.

The minesweepers resumed work again on the morning of 5 June. Five more mines were swept from the same area, but a sixth was struck by U.S.S. *Osprey,* who became the first casualty of the operation. The fleet made its way south at such good speed that they were within sight of France several hours before sunset. By 2145, when it was still light, at least one flotilla could pick out individual houses on the shore. They were well aware that they too could be seen, for some reason they were not attacked. All were relieved when the current changed direction and they could turn and sweep away from the coast. As the channels were swept, they were marked with lighted Dan buoys on either side, the entrance to the channels being marked by flashing lights.

Once the ten channels had been swept , it was once again time to close the French coast, this time in darkness. The requirement was now to sweep east/west in the British/Canadian sectors to clear the lowering and bombardment areas. For the American sector this meant clearing on a south east/north west axis. The British chose to have their lowering areas about seven miles offshore, while the Americans went for ten or eleven miles. When the landings took place the troops in the LCAs all suffered badly on the trip in, particularly the Americans with the extra distance to cover.

Many of the men who carried out this dangerous work were reservists, particularly fishermen. Theirs was a Cinderella service, which they called 'Harry Tate's Navy'. They performed their essential task so well that they that they earned the praise and admiration of all those who followed.

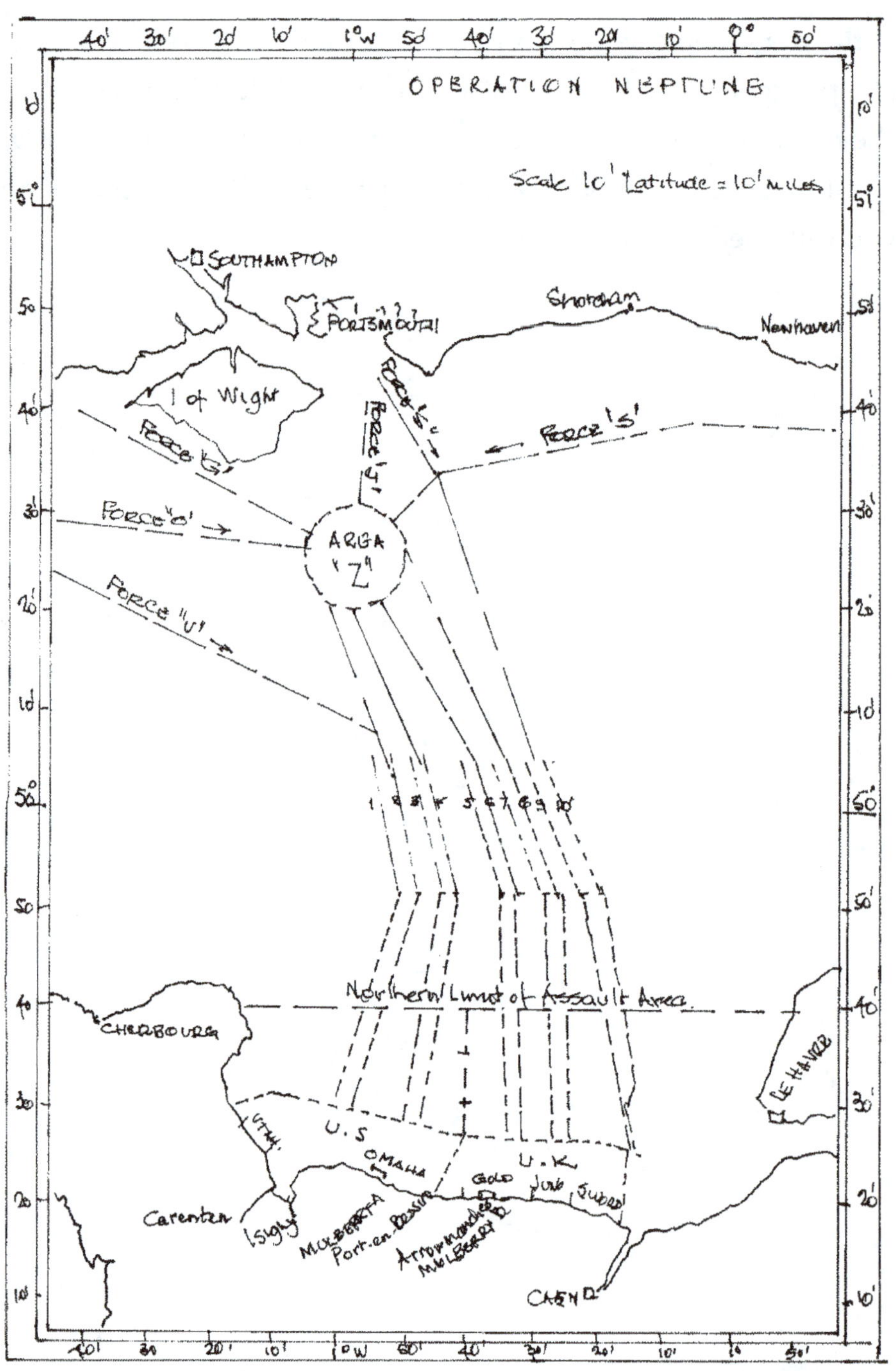
OPERATION NEPTUNE
Scale 10' Latitude = 10' Miles
SOUTHAMPTON
PORTSMOUTH
Shoreham
Newhaven
I of Wight
Force 'G'
Force 'J'
Force 'S'
Force 'S'
Force 'O'
Force 'U'
AREA 'Z'
1 2 3 4 5 6 7 8 9 10
Northern Limit of Assault Area
CHERBOURG
LE HAVRE
U.S
U.K
UTAH
OMAHA
GOLD
JUNO
SWORD
Carentan
Isigny
MULBERRY A
Port en Bessin
Arromanches
MULBERRY B
CAEN

The Landings

Admiral Ramsay's Order of the Day to the Allied naval forces, issued on 31 May said:

> Our task, in conjunction with the Merchant Navies of the United Nations, and supported by the Allied Air Forces, is to carry the Allied Expeditionary Force to the Continent, to establish it there in a secure bridgehead and to build it up and maintain it at a rate which will outmatch that of the enemy.

The target dates (D-Days), 5-7 June were chosen as the spring low water was close to the full moon. If the weather was adverse the fall-back was a fortnight later, but this would have been the time of the new moon. We now know that this was the time of the 'Great Storm'.

The troops returned to the ships they had exercised with up to early May and were greeted as old friends. Security was tight during the embarkation, which was completed by 2 June (Y+1).

The four **Sword** ships *Empire Battleaxe*, *Empire Broadsword*, *Empire Cutlass* and HMS *Glenearn* embarked their troops from the paddle steamers *Merstone* and *Shanklin*, while at anchor. Once the ships that had loaded alongside joined the others at their Solent anchorage. no communication with the shore was allowed.

The men enjoyed the time not spent cleaning weapons and kit by sunbathing and swimming in the early summer sunshine. Only the officers knew the site of the landings, the troops had been issued with maps without place names.

**The Green Howards boarding *Empire Lance* in Southampton.
Another LSI(L) can be seen, also embarking troops
© Crown Copyright: Courtesy Battlefield Historian**

The **Gold** and **Juno** ships had loaded at the Ocean and Empress
Docks in Southampton. Once loaded the Gold ships anchored in pre-
determined positions in the Western Solent, while those for the other
two Commonwealth beaches anchored at Spithead. The troops
destined for the initial assault at Omaha boarded from landing craft in
Weymouth Bay: those for Utah embarked in Tor Bay.

To recap:

Force **Utah** was comprised of US troops, plus a small unit of British commandos. In addition to a large fleet of LST and other landing craft their ships were: *Barnett, Bayfield* (HQ Ship), *Bienville* (Troopship), *Empire Gauntlet (LSI(L)), Excelsior* (Troopship), *Explorer* (Troopship) and *Joseph T Dickman* (Troopship). With the exception of the *Empire Gauntlet*, the ships are American.

The **Omaha** force was made up of US troops. Their ships were: *Achernar* (US), *Amsterdam, Anne Arundel* (US), *Borinquen* (US Troopship), *Charles Carroll* (US), *Dorothea L Dix* (US), *Empire Anvil, Empire Javelin, Exchequer* (US Troopship), *George S Simonds* (US Troopship), *George W Goethals* (US Troopship), *Henrico* (US), HMS *Invicta, Marine Raven* (US Troopship), HMS *Prince Baudouin*, HMS *Prince Charles*, HMS *Prince Leopold, Princess Maud, Samuel Chase* (US), *Susan B Anthony* (US Troopship), *Thomas Jefferson* (US), *Thurston* (US). Those with no nationality shown are British.

The British packet, now an LSI(H), *Ben-my-Chree* carried the US Rangers who were to storm **Pointe du Hoc**

The **Gold** ships were: *Cameronia* (Troopship), *City of Canterbury* (Troopship), *Empire Arquebus, Empire Crossbow, Empire Halberd, Empire Lance, Empire Mace, Empire Rapier, Empire Spearhead*, HMS *Glenroy, Leopoldville* (Belgian Troopship), *Louth* (Troopship), *Neuralia* (Troopship) *, *Pampas* (delayed), *Victoria*.

* Held back due to an administrative error. British except *Leopoldville*

Empire Arquebus carried C and D companies of the Royal Hampshire Regiment. *Empire Crossbow* (Captain Alexander Rodger) carried A and

B company of the Hampshire's. *Empire Spearhead* carried soldiers of the 231st Infantry Brigade and the 1st Battalion of the Dorset Regiment. As we saw above, the *Empire Lance* carried the Green Howards of the 69th Brigade.

The **Juno** ships were: HMS *Brigadier, Canterbury, Cheshire* (Troopship), *Clan Lamont, Devonshire* (Troopship), *Duke of Argyll,* HMS *Duke of Wellington, Isle of Guernsey, Isle of Thanet* (also reserve HQ ship), *Lady of Mann, Lairds Isle, Lancashire* (Troopship), *Llangibby Castle, Longford* (Troopship), *Mecklenburg* (Dutch), *Monowai* (New Zealand), HMCS *Prince David* (Canadian), HMCS *Prince Henry* (Canadian), HMS *Queen Emma, St Helier,* HMS *Ulster Monarch, Worcestershire* (Troopship). With the *Biarritz* in reserve.

The **Sword** ships were: *Empire Battleaxe, Empire Broadsword, Empire Cutlass,* HMS *Glenearn ,* HMS *Largs* (HQ ship), *Maid of Orleans, Princess Margaret,* HMS *Prins Albert* and HMS *Prinses Astrid.*

On 4 June the weather deteriorated with a strong wind and rough sea, all realised that there would be no crossing on that night. The weather would not have worried the bigger ships a great deal, though the soldiers may have suffered, but when they reached France, it would have been hazardous to launch the laden LCAs.

Later in the day came confirmation that the sailing would be on 5 June. Everyone was given the chance to write letters home, which were censored by the Chaplains.

On the *Maid of Orleans,* fondly known as The Maid, Captain Payne addressed all hands. He ended his rousing speech with:

Our job is to deliver the troops and keep on delivering. Joan of Arc, the Maid of Orleans, liberated France – the Maid will help to do the same, by the grace of God.

Then Major Menday explained the task for his troops. Everyone was said to be in high spirits, this was 'the real thing' after many months of exercises. On other ships, the mood was described as one of nervous anticipation.

Conditions on the 5th were still far from good but the barometer was rising. The wind was force five and would decline by one more point on the Beaufort scale before H hour (0630). In the early evening the sound of thousands of anchor chains being raised echoed across the Solent,; interspersed with the ship's bells marking each joining shackle as it came over the windlass. The slower Landing Craft had gone before.

From the Solent, the Gold ships sailed out past the Needles, while those for the other two beaches went via the Nab tower. They joined their swept channels at The Spout. No one but those on the lead ship knew that they were following the Decca Red lane and that the course alteration in mid-channel was triggered by reaching the Decca Green lane. Such was the secrecy that the Decca Navigator was switched off on the 7 June.

The ships arrived at their Lowering Positions (for the US Beaches, The Transport Area), at dawn. For the ships, carrying the American troops this was eleven miles off, while the British had elected for seven miles. Several commentators have remarked on this difference. The British troops had a rough trip to the beaches, but it was much worse for the Americans, who had an extra half hour of vomiting time. It has been suggested that the Americans wanted the big ships to be over the horizon; but the chart below shows that the Utah ships were as near as seven miles from Pointe du Hoc, where the horizon from the top would have been twelve miles. It was difficult to launch the LCAs in the prevailing condition, but there were no major calamities.

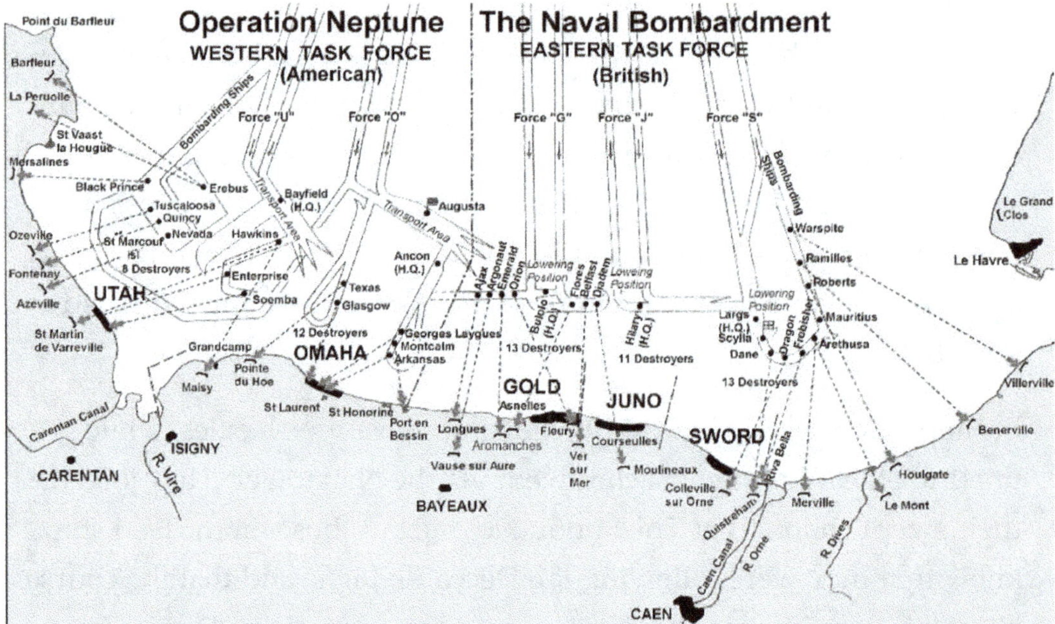

The landings were timed to coincide with low water, 0630 at Utah and just over an hour later at Sword. What no one had realised was that there was a strong alongshore current, which meant that many troops were put ashore more than a kilometre from the intended positions.

As the *Maid of Orleans* was approaching her lowering position the Norwegian Destroyer HMNS *Svenner*, blew up, broke amidships and sank beneath the waves: a shock for all who witnessed it. At 0540, The Maid anchored and within five minutes, her boats were manned. Her report says:

This proceeded in a most orderly manner, long practice having made each man familiar with his position in the different landing craft. As these were lowered at 0605, we of the ships company silently sent them our good wishes for it will be remembered that these specially trained Commandos had been with us over a period of many months and had grown to be part of the ship's company. There was a heavy sea running at the time and so it was with a sigh of relief that the craft were seen safely away without mishap, each soldier wearing full kit and extra ammunition.

Opposite the place where our craft landed was an enemy stronghold and the beach was swept from end to end by machine gun and mortar fire. Many men never reached the beach and one craft had a mortar bomb fall in the centre of it while packed with troops, killing two and wounding others. Although one air raid warning was sounded during the time the ship was anchored off the beaches, no enemy aircraft could have survived in the sky so dominated by our own aircraft. Five of our landing craft returned by 1030 and we were genuinely pleased to see them: one had struck a submerged obstruction and returned without any steering gear. The sixth craft had been lost by enemy action.

The weather was not good and, to hoist the landing craft, it was necessary to manoeuvre the ship with main engines to give them a lee, also to pour oil on the water to windward to assist them to get alongside. Most of the craft davits and lifting hooks were strained and damaged during this procedure. Whilst lying at anchor, heavy gunfire was experienced from shore batteries which appeared to be directed at us or at a convoy of tank landing ships which was passing close astern at the time.

This report is part of a long extract that John de S. Winser quotes in his book The D-Day Ships. I have tried to contact Mr Winser, but that has not been possible. He does not give a reference for the ships report and I have failed to track it down at TNA and the IWM.

There are a number of first hand reports on the internet, though sadly there is only one from a member of the Merchant Navy. 'Geobro' was Third Radio Officer on the *Lairds Isle*. He says:

> The MN Sparks were all sent on a weeklong signal course to a former school for young ladies I remember a plaque on the wall extolling us to "Be Modest and Preserve Our Honour"

On its website the famous Roedean Girls School, near Brighton, confirms that the Admiralty took over the school in April 1941. As HMS *Vernon*, they used it for torpedo, mine and electrical training. Roedean claims to be the only girl's school to have an Old Boys Association – Geobro would have been eligible!

He continued:

> It seems a contradiction in terms that merchant ships, manned by civilians, should play such a role. To steam into an enemy shore and land hundreds of invading troops can hardly be described as other than a hostile and aggressive act.

> These ships were formed into flotillas, with Lairds Isle being in Force J (for Juno beach). We carried half a battalion of Alberta Rifles (including the battalion's senior officers) and landed them in the Berniers/Courselles sur Mer region. Then returned at full speed back to Newhaven and took on board half a battalion of Royal Winnipeg Rifles, to land them in same manner. Exhilarating stuff, doing all this at 23 knots in a crowded channel. Then we yo-yo'd back and forth ad infinitum.

This was from 2008, sadly there are no posts from him after 2011.

As mentioned previously, there are two reports about *Empire Javelin*. On 2 June, she had returned to Portland to re-embark the troops of the 1st Battalion of the 116th Infantry Regiment, 29th Infantry Division and various support units. With 1,330 soldiers on board, and a complement of 250(?), the ship was very cramped. The bar was closed! 'A' Company was to be landed at Vierville sur Mer at 0530 (GMT +2) on 5 June. They were to be joined by two LCAs from HMS *Prince Charles*, carrying US Rangers. They sailed on the evening of 4 June, but were recalled to Portland after steaming for several hours. H-Hour was altered to 0630 on 6 June. They sailed again late on 5 June.

The landing craft were launched in the half-light of a grey morning, on to a nasty 'Channel Chop.' Several were damaged as the crowded boats collided. The craft from *Empire Javelin* and the other mother ships, made three trips that morning. Many of their stories can be read on www.combinedops.com.

As we saw above, oil was pumped by the ships, while they were recovering the boats. Where available this would have been vegetable oil, failing that lubricating oil could have been used. Oil effectively reduces the breakers, but coats craft, men, tackles and warps in oil. The recovery would have needed to be carefully planned. One of the most hazardous points was when the falls are re-engaged; if one end slips off, the boat will upend and could be flooded. Lifting all the boats on one side would have caused the ship to list, making the recovery of the boats on the opposite side even more difficult. So the recoveries would have alternated.

There were a number of serious injuries from swinging blocks. A Lieutenant Jimmy Green records that his Newfoundland coxswain 'was hit by a swinging block which threw him from one end of the boat to the other, splitting his forehead open to the bone'. Once the boat was safely hoisted aboard, the coxswain was handed over to the medical staff. There are no reports of crushed hands, though that was an ever present risk.

Green was so exhausted that he could not recall anything about the return trip. Fortunately, for him, and all on board, the merchant crew brought their ship home. Green's next recollection is of entering Plymouth harbour on the following day. As the first Landing Ship back in Plymouth, they received a hero's welcome. The anchored ships sounded their whistles and sirens. But their wounds were there for all to see. Six empty davits showed the boats that had not returned, a number of the others were badly damaged by shell fire.

Extracts from the article *'Princess Maud'*, courtesy of *www.combinedops.com:*

> The LCAs were constructed of wood with some armour plating for protection against rifle and machine gun fire. They were powered by two Ford V8 petrol engines driving twin screws with a cruising speed of seven knots. Her crew of four comprised a coxswain, mechanic, gunner and sheets man.
>
> That day, SS *Princess Maud* carried several hundred Yankee soldiers, mainly demolition men who were to land in advance of the main assault force to clear beach obstacles. These obstacles were designed to hinder the progress of the invading forces across the beaches and came in many forms including ramps, hedgehogs, stakes and element C *(substantial structures, also known as Belgian Gates).* These men had their own specialised craft to take them to the landing beaches. We would pick up our human cargoes from other troop carriers.

It was a very rough crossing and we hoped it would settle before we beached in our small, more vulnerable craft. As we neared France, Allied bombers with fighter escorts flew overhead to soften up the landing beaches in advance of our arrival. We could see a lot of enemy ack-ack fire in response. Unbeknown to us at the time, a few thousand paratroopers had already been dropped behind enemy lines.

We reached our rendezvous point (lowering position) about 03.00 hours on June 6th when the American troops of the 1st Battalion, 116th US Infantry, loaded into LCMs (Landing Craft Mechanised) secured alongside. At about 0400 hrs, we manned our craft and were lowered into the still rough waters. Manoeuvring our flat bottomed craft was not easy in the best of conditions but with 3 foot waves and a heavy swell it was a very tricky operation. Water sprayed over our boat as we headed for the *Empire Javelin*, a nearby LCA carrier. We were hoisted up to take on men of the US 5th Ranger Battalion.

Once fully loaded with our complement of troops we were lowered into the water and returned to the vicinity of our own ship where the LCMs were still loading the demolition teams. They were having a rough time as their craft were tossed up and down, banging against the ship's side with securing lines parting and being replaced. All the while, the men looked precarious climbing down scaling ladders with their heavy gear on their backs. The difference between the British and American loading procedures was dramatic in these rough conditions.

However, the British procedure was not without its problems. One of our craft, by then fully loaded with troops, was floundering and in danger of sinking. Although not apparent until the craft was back in the water, she had been holed during hoisting aboard the *Javelin* who refused to hoist her back! The coxswain kept his cool and circled *Princess Maud* until everyone, troops and crew, disembarked. Shortly after that, the LCA nose-dived beneath the waves.

There was little time for rest and recuperation since next day 4 new LCAs were delivered, replacing those lost or damaged and we sailed round to Portland for more troops.

LCA losses included: *Empire Arquebus* four out of eighteen; *Empire Battleaxe* eight out of 18; *Empire Broadsword* eleven out of 18; *Empire Crossbow* lost three out of 18; *Empire Javelin* six out of 18; *Maid of Orleans* one out of six; *Princess Maud* four, including those badly damaged. In all 90 were lost out of a total of 306.

Five convoys arrived between 1800 on the 6 June and 0830 on the following morning. The Americans regarded them as part of the Assault Force. As most, if not all, carried troops I have included them here.

Follow-up coaster convoy L1. All arrived Far Shore p.m. 6 June

Vessel	Flag	Beach	
Apricity	Br	Gold	
Broomlands	Br	Juno	
Dunvegan Head	Br	Sword	
Glengarriff	Br	Sword	
Heien	Nor	Utah	
Lottie R	Br	Omaha	
Marcel	Bel	Sword	
Mari	Nor	Omaha	
Monkstone	Br	Sword	
Northgate	Br	Gold	
Polglen	Br	Gold	
Sarnia	Br	Omaha	
Sedulity	Br	Juno	Cased petrol and Bailey bridging

Signality	Br	Juno
Skarv	Nor	Omaha
Skelwith Force	Br	Juno
Stanley Force	Br	Gold
Starkenborgh	Du	Utah
The President	Br	Omaha
Westland	Du	Sword

The Sword ships are listed as being loaded with priority stores; it is likely that the others were also.

Coaster convoy EWC1A arrived 7/0600

Vessel	**Flag**	**Beach**	
Crewhill	Br	Omaha	
Cushendun	Br	Utah	
Donaghmore	Br	Utah	Naval Stores
Erna	Du	Omaha	
Gem	Br	Utah	
Hawarden Bridge	Br	Utah	
Moelfre Rose	Br	Omaha	
Rockleaze	Br	Omaha	
Stuart Queen	Br	Utah	
Wallace Rose	Br	Utah	

Escorted by: HMS Goatfell and HMS Ryde

EBM2, 34 ships in total, only 24 are listed. This seems to have been the first US Liberty ship convoy for the Western Task Force. They each carried 5/600 troops and their vehicles:

Vessel	**Flag**
Benjamin Hawkins	Am

Bernard Carter	Am	
Charles M Hall	Am	
Charles Sumner	Am	
Charles Willson Peale	Am	
Edward W Scripps	Am	
Edwin Abbey	Am	Photo below
Eleazar Wheelcock	Am	
Ephraim Bevard	Am	
Ezra Weston	Am	Shelled 5 dead, ship saved.
Francis Harrington	Am	Mined at beach 5 dead, ship saved.
Frank R Stockton	Am	
George E Pickett	Am	
Henry W Grady	Am	
Horace Gray	Am	
Jedediah S Smith	Am	
John S Mosby	Am	
John Steele	Am	
Josiah Nelson Cushing	Am	
Oliver Wolcott	Am	
Robert E Peary	Am	
Robert L Vann	Am	
Stephen B Elkins	Am	
Walter Hines Page	Am	

Convoy ETM1, Liberties six for Juno & six for Sword arrived 7/0700

Samark (Br)	7,219	1943	
Samarovsk (Br)	7,219	1943	IWM Photos B 005215 (& B 5214?)
Sambut (Br)	7,219	1943	Shelled in Dover Strait, burnt out
Samdel (Br)	7,291	1943	

Saminver (Br)   7,210   1944   IWM photo A 23033

Sammont (Br)   7,219   1943

Samneva (Br)   7,219   1943

Samos (Br)   7,219   1943

Sampep (Br)   7,219   1943   *Daily Telegraph* correspondent

Samphill (Br)   7,219   1943

Samvern (Br)   7,219   1943

Samzona (Br)   7,219   1943

The coaster convoy EWC1B, arrived 7/0830 (H + 25 ½ hours)

Vessel	Flag	Beach
Activity	Br	Eastern Task Force
Ardgantock	Br	Eastern Task Force – Naval Stores
Avanville	Br	Sword
Dunvegan Head	Br	Sword
Durward	Br	Gold
Ebbrix	Br	Juno
Enid Mary	Br	Juno
Galacum	Br	Gold
Gladonia	Br	Sword
Holburn Head	Br	Sword
Ipswich Trader	Br	Gold
Kenrix	Br	Juno
Kyle Castle	Br	Gold
Kyle Queen	Br	Juno
Kylegorm	Br	Sword
Leoville	Br	Gold
Rockville	Br	Sword
Southport	Br	Juno

Stadion II	Nor	Juno
Teeswood	Br	Gold
Torquay	Br	Juno
Vestmanrod	Nor	Juno
Yewglen	Br	Gold
Yewpark	Br	Gold

The convoy identification letters were:

E from England (the return convoys being prefixed **F**).

Loading port: **B** - Bristol Channel, **C** - Cornwall & Devon, **P** – Portland & Weymouth, **T** - Thames, **W** – Wight (the Solent), **X** – Newhaven.

Then **C** – Coasters, **M** – Mechanised Transport, **P** – Personnel

British Liberty *Sammont* discharging off Normandy

There is a good IWM photo the British Liberty *Samarovsk* loading in London, Number B 005215. They also have two movie clips of this ship.

US Liberty *Edwin Abbey* discharging off the beach-head. ABS

Among the fleet that left the Solent Anchorage 19 E on 6 June were a number of British and French Tenders. Each had been on standby for the preceding three weeks, laden with navigational buoys, to replace the smaller Dan buoys laid by the minesweepers. With the Trinity House ships *Alert* (Captain T J White), *Patricia* (Captain R Goodman) and *Warden* (Captain J Le Good) were the French vessels *Andre Blondel* (Captain G Sherman) and *Georges de Joli* (Captain J R Meyrick). The Falkland Island Company's *Discovery II* was with this group, under the command of another TH Master (Captain J J Woolnough). *Alert* struck a mine on 16 June, while returning to Cowes after completing her task; she sank and hour and a half later.

The Trinity House sea pilots were equally busy. They piloted the ships in and out of the Solent and the Thames, with little respite. Some went on to Normandy, but it has not been possible to find any record of these trips.

The Post Office Cable ship, also *Alert,* sailed at 0001 on 9 June; her task was to lay telephone lines from the UK to Port en Bessin. Her sister *Iris* sailed with her from Southbourne; with the MOWT *Empire Flaminian* carrying additional cable and the barge *Leslie,* which was to land the shore end of the cable. The other Post Office cable ship that was involved was the *Monarch.* She was a victim of 'friendly fire' when shelled by the destroyer USS *Plunkett* and was towed back to Portsmouth.

Another group which included merchant ships were the boom carriers; many were HM ships. In response to an enquiry about the Runciman ship *Kirriemoor,* which was so employed, Hugh MacLean pointed out the ADM 1/15788 suggests that she was still HMS in August and September. He points out that there is no MN crew agreement for the vessel. I think it reasonable to assume that the other boom carriers were the same, though they may well have had merchant crews.

Follow-up convoys continued well beyond Operation Neptune,; again, the organisation was detailed. The only time that serious bottlenecks occurred was as a result of 'The Great Storm' in mid-June.

Normandy Convoys. (Data from: The Allied Convoy System - Arnold Hague)

Code	Normandy Invasion Convoys	1st Sailing	Last	Notes
BEC	Bristol Channel to France	June 1944	Oct 44	
EBC	Bristol Channel to France	June 1944	Oct 44	
EBM	Bristol Channel to France	June 1944	June 1944	motor transport
ECM	Falmouth, Cornwall to France	June 1944	early July	
ECP	Portland & Solent to Baie de la Seine	June 1944	Oct 44	personnel
EMM	Belfast to France	June 1944	July 1944	
EMP	Belfast to France	July 1944	July 1944	
EPM	Portland to France via Solent	July 1944	Sept 44	motor transport
EPP	Portland to France via Solent	July 1944	Sept 44	personnel
ETC	River Thames to France	June 1944	Oct 44	
ETM	River Thames to France	June 1944	Oct 44	motor transport
EWC	Spithead to Normandy	June 1944	June 1944	
EWL	Isle of Wight to France	June 1944	June 1944	LSIs & LCs +
EWM	Isle of Wight to France	Sept 1944	Oct 44	motor transport
EWP	Isle of Wight to France	June 1944	Sept 1944	personnel
EXP		June 1944	Oct 44	invasion
FBC	Baie de la Seine to Bristol Channel	June 1944	Oct 1944	
FC	France to western England	June 1944	July 1944	
FCP	France to western England	June 1944	July 1944	personnel
FPM	France to Portland Harbour	July 1944	Sept 44	motor transport
FPP	France to Portland Harbour	July 1944	August 44	personnel
FTC	France to River Thames	1944	1944	
FTM	France to River Thames	1944	1944	motor transport
FWC	France to Isle of Wight	June 1944		
FWL	France to Isle of Wight	1944	1944	landing craft
FWM	France to Isle of Wight	June 1944	July 1944	motor transport

FWP	France to Isle of Wight	June 1944	Sept 1944	personnel
FXP	France to British Isles	June 1944	Oct 44	
TMC	River Thames to France	June 1944	Oct 44	
TMM	River Thames to France	June 1944	Oct 44	motor transport
WAP		June 1944	Oct 44	invasion
WDC		Sept 44	Dec 44	invasion
WEC	Isle of Wight to France	Dec 44	May 1945	
WEL	Isle of Wight to France	1944	1945	landing craft
WFM		Oct 44	Nov 44	invasion
WMP	Isle of Wight to Arromanches-les-Bains	Nov 44	Dec 44	

How the Press saw it

A number of newspaper correspondents joined the merchant ships for the landings; this was probably the only time in any war that this happened. In total eighty men, and they were all men, were selected to cover the landings. Had they 'disappeared suddenly from their usual haunts' at the beginning of June this would have been a giveaway; so a practice run was carried out on the 22 May. The idea being that, when they again disappeared in early June, it would cause less of a stir. The takings in the Fleet Street pubs must have fallen sharply!

While great efforts were made to prevent women from going with the fleet, several succeeded. Probably the most famous was the American Martha Gellhorn, who stowed away on a Hospital Carrier. Another intrepid woman was British born Iris Carpenter. She had been refused permission to join the other correspondents covering the Mass Invasion of Europe, so she made the hazardous journey to the United States. There she was signed up by The Boston Globe and was accredited to the First United States Army. After another Atlantic crossing, she landed on D+4; but was soon in trouble for making her way to Cherbourg, without a military escort. Others who travelled across Europe with the First Army included Tania Long, Ann Stringer and Catherine Coyne.

Edmund Townshend, the correspondent of the Daily Telegraph, was given blue battledress, with a war correspondent's shoulder tabs and a big MN badge on the chest. 'I don't envy you, old man,' said the news editor. On D-Day, he sailed from the Thames aboard the British Liberty *Sampep*.

Townshend was a very experienced war correspondent, but, when he returned on Sunday 11 June, he wrote:

> Just back in port from the most dramatic and exhilarating voyage of my life, in my eight days afloat as one of the first war correspondents accredited to the Merchant Navy I have been given an insight into the comradeship, courage and unfailing good humour of this brotherhood of the sea. I shared with them the hazards of war.

On the morning of D-Day in the Straits of Dover he watched the ship astern (*Sambut*), take a direct hit, which cost twenty lives. Later (in another ship?), which was loaded with 800 tons of high-explosive ammunition, the chief officer observed, 'One enemy shell into this lot and you won't know where to look for your typewriter.' *Sampep* carried six hundred troops and their vehicles:

He concluded:

> Britain's Merchant Navy is living to-day its proudest hour. At last the chance has come for the men of the merchant ships to hit back. To-day the men are loading up again with fresh supplies of war material for their shuttle service to the armies in the field. © The Daily Telegraph

Peter Duffield, the 'Evening Standard Merchant Navy Reporter', joined what may have been the trooper *Neuralia* in the London Docks. Duffield said that there were 1,000 merchant ships manned by 50,000 Merchant Navy men, all volunteers. This must have been from a Ministry of Information handout, as the other correspondents give the same figures. .

From a British port on 7 June The Times, 'Special Correspondent with the Merchant Navy' wrote:

MERCHANT NAVY'S PART IN CHANNEL CROSSING
COMPLEXITY OF PREPARATION AND LOADING

Proudly prominent among the banners borne by the armada of liberation was the Red Ensign of the Merchant Navy, whose high duty it was to carry the allied fighting men and their machines to the last decisive battle-fronts. In doing so the Merchant Navy has redeemed a promise made as its ships cast off from Dunkirk and Narvik, Greece and Crete. ...

With our own Merchant Navy went the merchant ships and seamen of our allies. This civilian non-combatant service has had a glorious and costly acquaintance with all the hottest sectors in this world-wide war. It has shared set-backs and triumphs. ...

It carried a million men and thousands of tanks, aircraft and pieces of artillery, together with other stores to the Middle East before the sweep across North Africa frim El Alamein, It kept gallant Malta supplied. ...

The service endured with traditional fortitude the long grim battle of the Atlantic and went on to fresh heights of heroism in the fiercely contested Arctic runs to the Soviet Union.

He goes on to describe 'Previous Offensives,' continuing:

It was then that the Merchant Navy made its long-looked-for return to Europe; it carried the soldiers to Sicily and later to Italy. Now it has carried them to Hitler's 'western fortress.'

Years of planning and preparation, invention, and work preceded the sailing of this host of merchant ships. They were of all kinds. Passenger liners of graceful line and, in peacetime, pleasingly appointed, steamed with coasters of different shapes and sizes, cargo liners with ships specially designed for this greatest amphibious operation of all time. These last ships were designed in the Sea Transport Division of the Ministry of War Transport and built in California. .... Somewhat paradoxically, the mechanised army of to-day puts a terrific strain on transport services, though this is not hard to realise so far as the crossing of sea is concerned. ….

Besides special ships, special equipment had to be invented, such as the davits holding tiers of landing craft in the big troop-carrying ships. Hundreds of ships had to be specially fitted for the job. And then, before the Sea Transport Division of the Ministry of War Transport could go ahead with its master plan, details of all the ships to be engaged – the position of obstructions, space between decks, and so on – had to be collected and listed. ….

The loading plans of all the ships were prepared at a secret war-room in London: at the ports ship's officers cooperated and made improvements where possible. …. The technical men in the Ministry of War Transport and the Movements Directorate – many of them normally with well-known shipping lines – have evolved foolproof ways of packing in aeroplanes, tanks and other bulky stores, so that they are not likely to break away and charge about the holds

He then describes tactical loading at some length and writes several paragraphs about the part played by the coasters, 'V' articles and the 26,000 lives so far lost while serving on ships of the British Merchant Navy.

Following on from 'Coasters' Fine Record', he says:

Still smaller boats, the tugs, hundreds of them, also had a gallant and important part to play. Then there were the bigger ships, characteristically known officially as "ships landing infantry large"- in which troops of the allies made a cross-Channel trip. Also playing a part in these operations were hospital carriers and, for bringing casualties from the beaches, water ambulances.   © The Times

On a coaster The Daily Mirror man, John Hogan, wrote on 7 June 1944:

GREAT ARMADA STRETCHED OVER THE HORIZON

The guns have finally been checked, and the ship's clocks on board synchronised. Everything is now ready for the signal to hoist anchor and sail with our cargo of men, ammunition, petrol and mines.

Months of preparations have ended. Invasion talk, gossip and speculation are no more. Zero hour has come. For twenty four hours we have known that we will sail soon.

Imagine the biggest lake you know plastered with autumn leaves and you have a picture of what I can see from the salt sprayed bridge of our ship. Everywhere on the sea are steel ships. You can't get away from them, can't look anywhere without seeing long lines of troop ships, supply vessels, assault craft and warships – stretching away to faint blobs on the horizon.

Hundreds of ships ride at anchor in our convoy. Big ones that carried passengers, small ones that used to be grimed with coal dust, and strange ones that will race to the beachheads loaded with Commandos, tanks, bulldozers. I sailed for hours and still had miles to go before the leading vessel of this gigantic convoy came up within sight.

Today has been just another day on board this coaster, if you overlook the dozens of soldiers who swarm over the decks and live in a huge canvas tent slung on deck. Brown tents are to be seen everywhere. Sleek warships are alongside us, and minesweepers stretch out on the port side.

He goes on to talk about two members of the crew and their experiences evacuating troops from Dunkirk.

Then on 12 June, he wrote:

The men I sailed with to a Normandy beachhead are back in port again – enjoying a brief spell of shore leave before weighing anchor once more – washed and shaved for the first time in a week. In the little town where we celebrated our return and toasted the boys we left on the sandy beach, no one noticed the Merchant Navy men … the men who worked in flannels and vests under dive- bombing attacks and snipers' bullets.

They drank their beer unheeded in a bar crowded with civilians who talked of only one thing – the invasion. And when the evening ended they returned to their ship – to find her already loaded with hundreds of tons of bombs, shells and ammunition and awaiting orders to sail.

This is the life of the Merchant Navy in this huge Combined Operation. Protected only by light anti-aircraft guns, they are the most cheerful crowd in danger. They up their tin hats and swear steadily at the Mes and Ju 88s *(Messerschmitt and Junkers aircraft)*, and then grin as the bombs explode harmlessly in the 'suds' (?). That happened twenty five times one night while I was with them, and in the morning they had forgotten that ordeal to the extent that they never mentioned it. Such coolness is typical of the Merchant Navy.

On the way over, in between the watches they played Nine-Card brag on the mess-room table, oblivious to the roar of fighters and bombers above. Only when the kitty of 25s – won by the Major who landed on the beach next morning – was cleared did they think of the picnic ahead. And then, when we did drop anchor among the dozens of other vessels, they were disappointed by the lack of 'excitement.'

While we lay offshore a big landing-barge passed us, packed with about two to three hundred squatting Germans, including three generals with their suitcases already packed. On the beach French women were helping with the wounded. They had put on white frocks with red crosses. Two newcomers joined us during that first afternoon – two glider-pilots who obeyed orders to return to the beach immediately after landing.

He notes that the youngest member of the ship's crew was 17 year old
Charlie Brooker, who had hitch-hiked from Barnsley to Hull with only
(5?), shillings in his pocket and had a 'rare do' explaining things to his
mother. Charlie was one of a number of youngsters who joined the
Merchant Navy just in time for D-Day. …

> Now the men I lived with for a week – eating, sleeping and bomb-
> ducking on hundreds of tons of petrol and ammunition – are sailing for
> the beachhead again, with their neat pin-striped suits with the silver
> M.N. badges stowed away. They are wearing their patched flannels again
> – the battle dress of the Merchant Navy.
>
> © The Daily Mirror

On 12 June there is a piece written by a correspondent describing
what Fred Skinner, a Daily Sketch photographer, had told him of his
trip on 'the first ammunition ship to reach the beachhead'.

In The Daily Sketch on 7 June 1944, C W Kingdon wrote about the
vast panorama of ships which filled what must have been the Solent.
He said that it knocked the most impressive peacetime Naval Review
into a cocked hat. He saw something of the supremely important part
that the Merchant Navy was going to play. He also seems to have
been on one of the first convoys of coasters to follow the assault
troops to the invasion beaches.

Three of the first ships he saw were well-known peacetime packets,
packed with troops and carrying their landing craft slung from the
davits. He estimated that there were well over 4,000 ships of all kinds,
including troop ships with two rows of DUKWs slung one above the
other on the same set of davits.

The holds of the ship that he was on were filled with a general cargo of food, stores and spares for the troops and aircraft and hundreds of bicycles. There was also beer, rum, chocolates and tobacco.

On 8 June A D Divine, who may have been on the merchant LSI *Empire Spearhead*, wrote for the same paper. The journey home made and even greater impression on him than the hard moments of the landing. At two o'clock on 6 June his ship turned into the swept channel that led homewards. He said that there must have been a hundred L.S.Is of one type and another; then the faster personnel ships began to overtake them.

He listed some of the liners and flags he had seen. Then as one convoy passed, he could see the leading ships of the next coming over the horizon. It was 'almost too great for the eye, too heavy for the imagination.' He said that there had never been anything like it in history. He went on to say that there were 'not words enough to describe its complexity, not adjectives enough to summon up for those who were not there its staggering immensity.'

An article in The Daily Mail tells how a small tug made an unplanned trip to the beachhead. The reporter described her as 'dirty and gun-less' 'amid a fleet of invasion giants.'

On the eve of the assault a landing craft loaded with ammunition had engine trouble just outside the harbour. The tug *Empire Folk* was sent out to help. The master Arthur Hall, a 41-years-old north-country-man, had no idea the invasion was on when he got the call on Monday night (*5 June*).

The tug went alongside the immobilised craft and offered to take her back to port; only to be told 'you are going to take us to France.' Hall thought that his leg was being pulled, but the order was confirmed when 'the cruiser Scylla pulled up and Admiral Sir Philip Vian told us to take the L.C.T. in tow and head for France.' 'The commanding officer of the landing craft had to come aboard, because we didn't know the way through the mine-swept channels.' 'We didn't know it was an ammunition ship until he came aboard.'

With the help of contacts on the WW2 Talk Forum and elsewhere, the story has been pieced together. The *LCT 413* suffered engine failure off the Nab tower and was towed to Normandy by the *Empire Folk,* one of several tugs and salvage vessels stationed off Spithead and other assembly areas off the south coast. This ship had been built in Doncaster in 1942, as a river and estuary tug. She was less than one hundred feet long and her beam was restricted by the width of the lock between the shipyard and the river, making her less suitable for sea work. Two of her sisters also made it to France, one arriving on 8 June and the other on the 10th.

The Mulberry Harbours

When the Allies seized the Italian port of Naples on 7 October 1943 they found that it had been laid waste. The retreating Germans had not only scuttled ships throughout the port, they had added lighters, locomotives, cranes and trucks to the tangle. The harbour was covered with fuel oil and the power and water utilities had been wrecked. There was only one working berth. In the next few months, the British and American salvage crews removed a total of 160 wrecks from the harbour and its approaches.

Thus, they knew what to expect once they could capture the ports of Cherbourg and Le Havre. The massive defences at both harbours were part of the Atlantic Wall built by the Todt organisation, mostly with slave labour. The forces could not wait for the ports to be captured and cleared, so the British decided to prefabricate two complete harbours. Each was intended to be about the size of the harbour at Dover.

There is no agreement about who first came up with the idea. At a meeting after the Dieppe Raid in 1942, it is said that Vice-Admiral Hughes-Hallett proposed that if a port could not be captured one should be taken across the Channel. Even if a port could be captured, it was assumed that the Germans would again have made it un-useable with booby traps and block-ships before retreating.

The go-ahead was given at the Quebec conferences in 1942 and 1943. Winston Churchill, who also claimed to have first thought of the idea during the Great War, wrote in one of his famous directives on 'one side of one sheet of paper':

Piers for use on beaches – They must float up and down with the tide. The anchor problem must be mastered – let me have the best solution worked out. Don't argue the matter. The difficulties will argue for themselves.

With the fall of France in 1940 the South coast ports became unusable because of the constant threat of enemy action or invasion. The loss of the use of Southampton was a particular blow; though it did mean that the port was able to play a key role in D-Day. To relieve the congestion elsewhere two ports were built from scratch, at the Gareloch (Military Port No 1) and Cairnryan (Military Port No 2). The Royal Engineers, with the Pioneer Corps, began the preliminary dredging work late in 1940 and the first deep-sea ships used the facilities in July 1942. Not only did they build the two deep-water ports, they also built the back-up road and rail links.

Many of the American troops and their equipment were landed there in the next eighteen months. The design and construction experience that was gained was carried forward to the construction of the Mulberry Harbours.

The site of the American harbour (Mulberry A) at St Laurent was on an open sandy beach with a slope of approximately 1 in 100. The tidal range was around 20 feet (~6 Meters) at springs and the maximum tidal stream was 2.8 knots, setting along the shore. The British harbour, at Arromanches, was enclosed by low rocks to the west and the Calvados reef about two miles out. The spring tidal range was 21 feet and the maximum current 2.3 knots.

Both harbours were exposed to winds from the north-west through to the east. As gales were thought unlikely during the summer the components were designed to withstand winds of up to force six. Shelter was to be provided by D + 4 and the target date for substantial completion was D + 14: the intended working life was set at ninety days.

At all states of tide there was to be discharge space at Mulberry A (with Mulberry B in brackets), for: seven (eight), Liberty type ships on buoys; 15 (20) coasters alongside; about 400 tugs, ferries and other craft. In addition, temporary shelter was to be available for one thousand small craft from other beaches! This required an enclosed area of 1,400 acres with 18 feet depth at high water, almost twice the size of Dover or Gibraltar.

The layout chosen for the Mulberry Harbours was for a number of floating pier heads, at which ships would discharge, to be connected to the shore by long roadways supported by pontoons. To seaward were to be block ships and concrete caissons. Together these formed the outer breakwaters, protecting both the floating quays and the beached coasters. The Gooseberry block ships were to form detached moles (breakwaters that are not connected to the shore). They were to reinforce the Phoenixes, which also formed the breakwaters at the harbour ends, extending to the shore.

The Gooseberries were to be made up of four warships and 53 merchantmen. With the exception of the French battleship *Courbet,* these were able to reach their destination under their own power. The British were to provide 31 and the Americans 22. The Ministry of War Transport found it extremely difficult to source this number of merchant ships, without reducing their cargo fleet. Useless ships could provide about one third of the total, and ships that were slow and in need of constant repair another third. The remainder had to be found by allocating ships that were still useful.

Lobnitz of Renfrew undertook the design of the pier heads. They used spud piles to anchor the barges, as they used on the dredgers they had built for many years, hence the name Spud Piers. A spud leg was built into each corner of the barge. When they were raised, the unit could be towed like an ordinary barge. Once on site the legs were jacked down; either to anchor the barge firmly in position, allowing it to float up and down with the tide, or to raise the barge clear of the water. The same idea was used when offshore oil drilling started after the war. See IWM photograph B 007236, coaster *Flathouse* alongside spud piers

Among those who were involved in the design of the roadways were the Welsh civil engineer Hugh Iorys Hughes, Professor J. D. Bernal and Major Allan Beckett of the Royal Engineers. As Beckett's design was the only one of three that survived a storm at the test site in Wigtownshire, it was adopted and given the code name 'Whale'. The construction of a total of ten miles was put in hand at sites all over Britain.

The Whale piers connected the pier heads to the shore. The roadways were made from flexible bridging units with a span of eighty feet, mounted on steel or concrete pontoons. These 'Beetles' were moored by wires attached to 'Kite' anchors (similar to CQR or Plough anchors) designed by Major Beckett. These anchors had such high holding power that few could be recovered at the end of the War.

At some point, the Admiralty intervened; designing anchors was not for soldiers, even ones as clever as Allan Beckett. They decided they would engineer an outer floating breakwater, which they would anchor 'properly'. In the event these Bombardons broke loose in the, so-called, Great Storm. It was said that the Bombardons that did not sink caused more damage to the British harbour at Arromanches, than the storm.

The design of the main breakwater caissons were not finalised until October 1943; construction began immediately. In all 147 were ordered for D-Day, a further 66 were added later. There were six types of these Phoenix units, ranging in size from 1,672 tons to 6,044 tons. They were to be: seaworthy and towable, easy and quick to plant, stable once planted, and designed so that they could be built in the time available. This last requirement had to be met without putting further strain on the already overextended shipyards, or the bridge builders and other structural engineering firms who were busy building landing craft. The units were swim ended - the bow and stern were sloped from just above the waterline to the base. While this improved the towing speed, some claimed that it would increase the scour between the units once they were laid, but this did not seem to be so.

Construction sites were situated all over southern England. Little used Southampton became one of the construction centres, with units being built in dry-docks and on beaches throughout the Solent. On the banks of the Thames, huge craters were dug, separated from the river only by a narrow strip of land. Several units were built in these, even though they needed to be pumped constantly. Once the structures were buoyant, the craters were flooded and the strip of land removed; the structures were floated out and completed elsewhere. The East India Dock and the Surrey South Dock were pumped out and the now unsupported walls of the East India Dock partly collapsed, but work continued! Other units were built in places as far afield as Hartlepool, Birkenhead and Grimsby

All the famous civil engineering firms were involved, including Balfour Beatty, Costain, Cubitts, Henry Boot, Mowlem, Nuttall, Robert McAlpine and Taylor Woodrow. So were many lesser-known firms, such as Southampton Steam Joinery, who had already turned their hands to assembling Fairmile MLs on the banks of the River Itchen. The completed Phoenix units were towed by tugs to shallow water between Dungeness and Selsey Bill, where they were 'parked' by ballasting them down on the seabed. Those constructed in and around London were parked in the Thames Estuary.

The quantities of material needed for the caissons alone included: over half a million cubic yards of concrete, 66,000 tons of reinforcing rod, nearly one and a half million cubic feet of timber and almost one hundred miles of wire rope. At its maximum, the labour force employed on the caissons totalled about twenty thousand; they came from all over the country.

During April and May, it could be seen that the construction programme was falling behind schedule and many units were being delivered late. Problems with fittings included inadequate towing connections with badly located fixing points. Towing bridles had not been provided; this did not present a problem for the large ocean going tugs, but it did for the smaller tugs who normally only worked in harbours and who did not carry their own towing gear.

When it came time to mobilise, the first problem was the chronic shortage of tugs. Presumably, the Army had intended to use the small prefabricated TID tugs that had been built for the MOWT, but these were not up to the task of towing even the smaller Phoenix units across the Channel.

In August 1943 the Combined Chiefs of Staff Advisory Committee reported that fifty 750 BHP and forty 1,000 BHP tugs would be required for the Mulberries. A further forty tugs were needed for other Neptune requirements. A MOWT census showed that tugs could only be found by withdrawing a fifth of the harbour berthing tugs and suspending all coastal towage. These needed to be supplemented by one third of the rescue tug fleet and a quarter of the Admiralty dockyard tugs. Together this would provide only 65 of the required tugs and it could only be a short-term solution. It was thought that the others would need to come from the United States, but only rescue tugs could steam across the Atlantic, the smaller units had to be carried by cargo ships. There are some dramatic photographs of Liberties with such deck loads, from this time.

A new body known as COTUG was hurriedly set up on the 24 May; headed by Admiral Edmond Moran USNR, it reported directly to ANCXF. There were not enough tugs in the country, however, to satisfy all Civil, Naval and Military demands for their services. By the end of May only 48 out of 72 large and four of the 44 small tugs were available. Admiral Ramsay directed that 'Mulberry constituted a vital part of the whole operation' and this 'must govern decisions as to the extent that tug assistance could be provided for other purposes'.

When the time came to re-float the Phoenix units further shortcomings were revealed: the intake valves were too small to allow units to be sunk rapidly enough to be positioned accurately; the pumping gear supplied was inadequate for this purpose; and the apertures for the de-watering pipes were not big enough for the flanges. The Admiralty again intervened, but most of those who carried out the work for them were civilians. The need could only be met by diverting salvage vessels to site. None of the salvage fleet earmarked for the landings could be used, so many of the smaller units kept back for work on the UK coast had to undertake the task. Twenty ships were assigned as pump vessels and two others as accommodation ships as some of the little vessels were no more than day boats.

The Risdon Beazley managed *Longtow* and *Roselyne* were sent to Selsey. There about sixty sections were parked. Each had to be pumped out and re-floated with the crews racing one another to ensure that they did not end up with the unit listing towards them, which would mean more work for that ship's crew. With all the haste and the rivalry, there were a few crushed arms and legs. Once the units were re-floated, the pumps were stripped off and the units handed over to the 'pongees' *(probably pongoes – a seaman's name for soldiers, actually an African ape).*

The other pump vessels were: *Barensz, Mies, Noord-Stad* and *Vida* (Dutch schuyts), *Dapper* and *Doria,* (two small coastal barges), *Empire Demon, King Lear, Lamb, Richard II, Swift, Thames Coast, Tordenskjold* (Nor.), *Urmajo, Watercock, Yewdale* (a collier), *Zeehond and Zeus* (Dutch schuyts?).

All but a handful were handed over to the transit tugs. In all 166 tugs were eventually employed, some flew the White Ensign of the Royal Navy, while others flew the Red Ensign of the civilian service and a few the Dutch tricolour. The tug shortage was never completely solved, which meant that the tug crews became increasingly exhausted as the build-up continued.

Towage was to begin on D-day from Selsey, the Solent, Dungeness, and Portland. Tows were not to cross latitude 50° North before noon on D plus 1. Outward and homeward channels were reserved for the tugs and their unwieldy tows; with an average towing speed of only five knots they were at the mercy of the Channel currents and even more vulnerable to attack than the other ships. The components of the Mulberry harbours were to arrive at both sites daily from D + 2 to D + 17, with the intention that the harbours would be complete by D + 18.

The block ships were the first units to mobilise. The ships had been stripped of everything of value by the frugal British. Holes had been cut in their watertight bulkheads and they had been wired for scuttling charges. Their only identifying marks were numbers painted on their sides.

The bulk of the ships assembled at Methil, on the east coast of Scotland, from where they sailed in CORNCOB convoys on 23 May. Progress was painfully slow and, as their maximum speed was just over five knots, getting safely through the Pentland Firth was an achievement in itself. One ever-present fear was that two of these unmanageable ships would collide. Had they done so, they would have sunk quickly. After three days they reached Oban, on the west coast of Scotland. At this time there were 56 Gooseberries;, with them were ten tugs, with a number of escorting Corvettes.

At the final convoy conference, the convoys were routed to the Bristol Channel. The Masters realised that this would not be their final destination when they were issued with sealed orders. On sailing they formed up in three convoys, each of two columns. The first formed of 22 British and Allied vessels, the second the American ships and the third those that were so decrepit that they might have held the others back.

CORNCOB I (British, unless marked otherwise)

Becheville, Bendoran, Courageous (US), *Dover Hill, Empire Bunting, Empire Defiance, Empire Flamingo, Empire Moorhen, Empire Tamar, Empire Tana, Flowergate, Georgios P* (Gr), HMS *Alynbank*, HMS *Durban, Innerton, Manchester Spinner, Mariposa, Modlin* (Po), *Panos, Parklaan* (Du), *Saltersgate, Sirehei* (No), *Vera Radcliffe, West Cheswald* (US). The six Empire Vessels had all been taken over from other flags.

CORNCOB II (American, unless marked otherwise, * = joined convoy in Irish Sea)

Artemas Ward, Benjamin Contee*, David O Saylor*, Flight-Command** (Pa), *Forbin* (Br, ex Fr), *Galveston*, George Wasson*, James Iredell*, James W Marshall* (ex Cardiff), *Mat W Ransom*, Olambala*, Potter*, Victory Sword*, Vitruvius*, West Grama, West Nohno*, Willis A Slater*, Wilscox**.

CORNCOB III. *Aghios Spyridon* (Gr), *Elswick Park, Empire Waterhen, George W Childs* (US), H.Neth.M.S. *Sumatra*, HMS *Centurion, Ingman, Lynghaug* (No), *Njegos* (ex Yug), *Vinlake, West Honaker* (US).

The French battleship *Courbet* was towed from Plymouth via Weymouth Bay by the rescue tugs HMRT *Growler* and HMRT *Samsonia*.

The escorting tugs were the MOWT's *Empire Aid, Empire Doris, Empire Henchman, Empire Humphrey, Empire John, Empire Jonathon, Empire Larch, Empire Rupert* and *Empire Winnie* (most with Corncob III).

By this stage of the war the merchant ships were well accustomed to maintaining close formation, but on this voyage they kept as far apart as possible, everyone realising what disaster would result from a collision. Both the *Empire Tamar* and the *Dover Hill* sheared across the convoy, but were able to resume their stations. *Empire Winnie* took *Empire Defiance* in tow when she suffered 'irreparable' machinery damage, but her engineers were as defiant as their ship and after seven hours, she was again under her own steam. *Innerton* also needed a tow from the *Empire Rupert*.

They arrived at Poole Bay on the 5 June, having been turned back in the Bristol Channel, because of the one-day postponement of the landings. The two rescue tugs had a difficult time holding the *Courbet* for a day in Studland Bay. At 1600 on D-Day, two of the three CORNCOB convoys sailed to 'the Far Shore' on their final voyage. One reached the French coast at 1400 and the other at 1600 on D + 1. CORNCOB III sailed mid-day on the 7 June.

As they arrived a start was made on planting the block ships, the programme called for one unit to be scuttled every forty minutes. Gooseberry One, made up of nine US flag ships, was to protect Utah beach. It ended somewhat out of line, perhaps understandably, as it was laid under enemy gunfire, it also had an unintended gap. Gooseberry Two was to be laid off Ste Laurent, using an old British Battleship and eight US flag and five Panamanian flag cargo ships. This breakwater was to protect the eastern entrance to Mulberry A, but it was planted with insufficient overlap and two gaps. This may have contributed to the disaster that befell the harbour during the 'Great Storm'.

Gooseberry Three was made up of fifteen cargo ships; eight were British and the balance came from various European Allies. This was to be off Gold Beach, protecting the two entrances to Mulberry B.

Gooseberry Four, of ten ships, was to provide shelter to Juno Beach: it included one Greek and one Belgian ship. It was somewhat misaligned, so that it provided less shelter than intended.

Gooseberry Five was to be on the extreme left flank of the British sector; it was made up of six British cargo ships and three old Allied warships. It was not laid to plan, because of changes required by the Assault Force Commander, and provided less protection than intended.

The first Phoenix tows set off from Selsey at 0200 on D + 1. They were expected to make three knots, giving a passage time of 72 hours. In the event the tugs managed an average of 4½ knots. The first were planted at Mulberry A on D + 3 and at Mulberry B at D + 2. The planners had provided for a 20% loss rate, but only three units were lost; two due to enemy action and the third from an unknown cause. One of the tugs, HMS *Sesame*, was torpedoed by an E-boat; only three of her crew survived, to be picked up by the HMS *Stormking*. Her tow was delivered to France by the *Stormking*, whose crew claimed that this was her third delivery in a day; the other being a Phoenix apparently abandoned by a US tug.

On the evening of D-Day the first four Bombardon tows sailed from Portland. Twelve tugs were allocated for this task. Groups of four tugs, each towing two Bombardons, were sailed at 1600 on the following four days. These units towed well and none were lost in transit. Half of the tugs were MOWT Empire tugs, the others were tugs that the navy had requisitioned.

Two convoys of mooring vessels sailed at around the same time. Mooring Force A was part of convoy EWC1A and Mooring Force B in convoy EWC1B. They were each made up of two HM net layers. Three of these were requisitioned from the Southern Railway fleet, six boom defence vessels, three trawlers and a larger merchant cargo vessel as a boom carrier. A further three cargo vessels and three trawlers sailed later.

The first Whale tows sailed in the early hours of D + 2, arriving on the Far Shore 24 hours later. Assembly of the centre pier at Mulberry B began on the day after arrival. Work in Mulberry A was delayed by three days when land mines were discovered at the site. By D + 5, four Whale tows, with six hundred yards of roadway, had been lost during the crossing. On the next day, it was decided that these tows should not sail in more than a force four wind in a south west quadrant. Initially the roadways were towed in 480 ft. lengths, but a subsequent halving of the length did not seem to reduce the losses.

The Crews

Tony Hodge

The late Tony Hodge left the Royal Merchant Navy School at sixteen having been accepted as a Writer by P & O (Peninsular & Oriental). He joined the office staff in September and was due to join their *Narkunda* in the autumn. Arriving at the office in late November, he found that he was no longer required, as the company had lost five of their 16 liners in the North African landings. He applied to the Ministry of War Transport, but as a seventeen year old was rejected for service as a PO Writer on Armed Merchant Cruisers. He felt that this rejection may have done him a good turn as the AMCs had earned the nickname of Armed Merchant Coffins.

He was taken on by the Admiralty Salvage Department, joining a small unit in Grimsby as Writer/Storekeeper. A far cry from P&O. Early in 1944 Tony Hodge joined the Risdon Beazley managed A.S.V. *Gallions Reach* at Immingham.

Like several of the requisitioned units, this ship had been built as a self-propelled mud hopper. Her owners were the PLA, as one of a number of craft that were employed carrying dredging spoil from London River to the dumping grounds in the estuary. She had been equipped with the pumps, wires and even Polar Blasting Gelignite that made her suitable for salvage work when the need arose.

In May, they signed 'V' Articles to sail for the 'Mass Invasion of Europe'. They left the Humber on the 19 May and anchored off the Medway, joining convoy ETC 5 on 9 June. Before leaving the Humber, they had a visit from Army Intelligence, who especially warned them

not to keep diaries. As Tony says, it became apparent after the war
that their own senior officers disobeyed these instructions.

Gallions Reach* before she was modified. *Source unknown

Tony's recollections of *Gallions Reach* at Arromanches are included in
full:

The convoy regrouped off Portsmouth on the night of the 10 June and we
sailed for Normandy, a bright moonlight night, the sort that during the
blitz was referred to as a Bomber's Moon and it turned out that the E-
boats from Le Havre liked it too. We felt rather naked when the firing
started as one of the escort had a breakdown and had to return to
Portsmouth and one of the others was hit although it still continued
firing. The convoy was in two lines and a small tanker on our port side
was torpedoed, exploded, and showered us with oil. At least two people
survived as we saw red life-jacket lights in the water and though we
couldn't do anything I think an escort picked them up astern. Meanwhile
we were happier when we had another ship abeam between the action
and us.

We got to our designated anchorage in what was being turned into
Mulberry Harbour and already a line of old ships had been sunk and the

huge concrete caissons were being sunk to extend the breakwater. This being my birthday I had a tot of rum, the first time I remember tasting it. At that time the Royal Navy ratings got a tot of rum every day but we had just one gallon jar on board for a sweetener after cold or hazardous work but we soon found out that we could replenish our stock very easily!

My feelings that day were of being very proud to be part of such an endeavour. I believe that there were something like five thousand ships spread out along the beach head from battleships to small tankers and workhorses like us and in between them a host of landing craft, launches and DUKWs scurrying around. Landing ships and Landing craft were running up on the beach discharging men, guns, tanks, ambulances, and lorries with everything bound inland.

A battleship, the *Rodney* I think, was offshore shelling targets ashore with the shells passing over our heads so there was quite a bit of noise but there was very little enemy air activity during the day. To avoid being opened fire on by trigger-happy gunners all allied Aircraft had, at the very last moment, been painted with very distinctive black and white stripes. Friendly Fire was very well known then too!

The nights were very noisy as German aircraft tried to fly over the beachhead to drop mines and presumably to gather intelligence. All gunnery officers had been allocated a section of the sky into which to fire, i.e. creating a box barrage. With all H.M. Ships including special AA Cruisers firing and as all units comprising the breakwater had Bofors Guns it really was a Brock's Benefit, and with smaller 20 mm tracer shells cross-crossing the sky it was really beautiful. Our Radio Officer, Dave Wicks, a wartime recruit who had been studying at the Royal Academy of Art, was apt to be so entranced that on at least one occasion he stood out on the deck wearing only his underpants and a steel helmet working on a scratchboard with the odd shell splinters clanging on the deck and spitting into the water alongside the ship. I wonder if he ever showed his sketches – some years after the war I did go to the Royal Academy show and saw one of his line drawings but it was not of the beachhead.

There was one German plane that used to come over during the day on reconnaissance and we rather admired his cheek as he flew very low, too low for the gun battery on the cliff to depress their guns and the ships could not fire at it without hitting other ships or troops ashore. One day, at low tide, gunners had 20 mm guns mounted on lorries down on the beach and as we watched they caught him as he made his run. There was a brief cheer and then someone said "Poor sod" our tribute to him and we all went back to work rather quietly.

About this time there was a sudden flurry of air activity concentrated over the beachhead, fighters overhead instead of flying to the front inland and naval ships up to something and we found out soon afterwards that King George VI had paid a visit. It was said that Churchill had told the King that he would go over on D Day but the King said 'If you go – I go' which put a stop to that.

Apart from the noise from the AA guns at night there were constant patrols through the anchorage dropping small charges against midget subs and frogmen. I never heard of these intruders having any success inside the anchorage though they did sink at least one destroyer – the *Quorn* – outside the anchorage. The effects of these small depth charges when one was laying in one's bunk was like someone hitting the bulkhead next to you with a very large hammer so I preferred to sleep on deck as the weather was quite warm.

The weather however changed again and we had an on-shore gale blowing. We had at one stage both anchors down and we were steaming up to them – every sailor's nightmare to be caught on a lee shore. The off-loading of stores into DUKWs stopped and very little could be landed on to the beach or via the temporary metal causeways which were being constructed. We had the worst case of seasickness that I had ever seen at the time. The lad would not go down below so we sat him in a lifebuoy and lashed him to a funnel stay otherwise he would have gone overboard via the scuppers and wash port and it was patently obvious that he didn't care anyway.

As soon as the weather moderated slightly, we set out to help ships in trouble and I remember particularly going to the Tank Landing craft adrift in the Channel that was very low in the water and listing badly. It had a couple of canvas topped 3 tons lorries on board and the soldiers were huddled on top of them and looked very pleased to see us. It's nice to know that you're wanted!

The success of the whole Invasion was in jeopardy as very little supplies could be landed. One ammunition ship had been blown ashore and was sitting upright on the sand and our Captain, Lawrence, was ordered to steam alongside her at high water and beach ourselves. He was not a happy Cappy as he said, he was told to do something that he'd spent all his life trying to avoid! Having bilge keels we managed to tie up alongside her and dry out and the Royal Engineers used our derricks and winches to off load the ammunition over on to lorries on the beach at low tide and into DUKWs when the water rose. This went on through the night under floodlights, which were only turned out when enemy planes were overhead. In spite of having been under water the shells went straight up to the front line, which certainly wouldn't have pleased any Armament Supply Officer under normal circumstances!

Before we left Arromanche Capt. Lawrence was awarded the D.S.C., and I think it was probably this episode that gained him it. He, of course, described it as a 'Roti' gong (i.e. came up with the rations)

Shortly after this was the big raid of 450 Lancasters on Caen where the British, facing the main concentration of German Armour, were being held up. With the naked eye we could see the planes suddenly rise as they released their bombs. There was something very unreal about drinking mugs of tea on deck and watching all this happen and I was reminded of this feeling when I turned on the T/V on Sept 11th and watched the events unfold at the Twin Towers of New York. The thought that you ought to be horrified at knowing that people are being killed and yet feeling very detached. There was some AA fire and we saw one Lancaster limping home and losing height and counted the crew bailing out. When six had left the aircraft one of our lads said that there was one chap still left and the pilot bravely waited until the plane had cleared the anchorage and then he too jumped and was soon picked up.

I got ashore occasionally, once on the back of a motorcycle driven by a mad Canadian R.N.R. Officer attached to us as Salvage Officer. I wasn't happy in the lanes torn up by tank tracks and shell holes and even less happy when I saw a Military Police notice saying that we were in sight of enemy observation posts. I don't know where we went or why – all I remember is hanging on for dear life and clutching a couple of round boxes of Camembert Cheese. I'm not awfully keen on Camembert but having been too young for such tastes before the war I still look on them as the first fruits of victory.

Another time ashore I met a matelot who told me that he was in H.M.S. *Albatross* which I think was a converted Seaplane Carrier and he told me that his captain was trying to get them all killed, refusing to up anchor when being shelled by shore batteries and 88s in Sword Area, the eastern extremity of the Beach Head. This Captain had rebuked an officer who ducked down behind a canvas dodger when a shell came over saying that he should behave like a gentleman. When he conducted a funeral service of some of his men that had been killed he said that he envied the men killed in action and trusted that the rest of the ship's company felt the same! I thought that this was just a matelot's whinge or at least an exaggeration, but in 1994 I saw a detailed account basically confirming this and even named the Captain. I only hope that the relatives of men killed on board her never read this account.

During the storm the harbour that the Americans had built at Port-en-Bessin, which was in an exposed position, was wrecked as in their quest for speed in construction they had not put the specified number of anchors out. The units they salvaged were added to the British harbour and some of their vessels used the anchorage. About a month after our arrival at Arromanche and having sustained no damage except a few shell splinters in our funnel we were minding our own business in Mulberry Harbour when an American Tank Landing Ship with the tide under her stern careered through the anchorage and hitting us a glancing blow carried most of our bow ramp away and we were sent ignominiously home to Southampton for repairs.

Tony became a Purser in the Royal Fleet Auxiliary and later a Chief Purser in the Union Castle Line.

Peter Oliver joined the Risdon Beazley managed SV Help, as a Deck Boy, in March 1944. An extract from his reminiscences:

There was a lot of shipping and although this seemed to be increasing we took only a casual interest in it. We saw no significance when we were moved the few miles west to Portland. It was not until the 29th May, we became aware we were a tiny part of a large armada of ships. Within a few days it became clear that the invasion of Normandy was imminent.

It is believed that foul weather delayed matters somewhat and it remained a considerable handicap when the invasion of Normandy was launched on June 6th.

In total there were five beaches, two of which named Omaha and Utah were the responsibility of the American forces. It soon became clear that we were seconded to the Americans with the responsibility of helping (to) maintain a clear passage to the beaches for the armed forces.

For a number of days we saw nothing of the beaches. We got scanty information of a number of horror stories relating to the assault of Omaha beach and the apparent loss of many US lives from enemy fire and from drowning. We laid off the beaches for a few days and nights but there was much to do assisting other craft where necessary.

At sea shipping is vulnerable to enemy aircraft, torpedoes and magnetic mines. The Navy must have done a great job of mine sweeping, we encountered no enemy shipping and during the day there was a complete absence of enemy aircraft. At night there was the occasional visit from German planes which mainly dropped flares to light up the scene below. This at least afforded our gunners target practice with their attempts to shoot down the flares. It was also added excitement for me as with an Oerlikon gun situated immediately above my bunk, sleep was impossible so I remained on deck helping when I could and on occasions helped with the loading of one of the guns.

Our two gunners were great guys. One a Londoner known as Tosh who idolised the Glen Millar band and one of their famous numbers which he had renamed the settee serenade. The other, Taffy from Wales, who a couple of years earlier had been torpedoed when in a convoy to Russia , spent around 20 days in an open boat in the Arctic Sea and as a consequence had almost completely lost his voice.

The scene at Omaha beach was, we understood, horrific and at one time utter chaos. There were bodies in the water and many more beneath the surface. Our divers had the difficult task of working on or alongside scores of sunken vessels, with many bodies visibly trapped inside the wreckage. The ashen faces of the divers on their return to the surface was testimony to the horrors witnessed ~ without doubt justification for the awards they later received.

Utah beach was an entirely different situation with hardly any enemy resistance. The beach was cleared completely in a matter of days and quickly filled again with every conceivable allied weaponry. We moved well away and anchored where the waters were clear and clean and it was somewhat quieter. The sun shone it was warm and we took every opportunity to swim. I burst an ear drum trying to emulate the good swimmers around us with what we called the jack-knife dive. My right arm was badly gashed on a sharp object beneath the surface. We remained in the area until the fall of Cherbourg on the 27th June, just three weeks after D-Day.

It is recorded that in only the first 24 hours of D-Day America lost no fewer than 31,465 men.

Peter became the Managing Director of an insurance company.

Sydney Day was with Risdon Beazley for much of the war.

For the salvage vessels that remained on the UK side, times were equally busy; *Longtow* was then based in Dover and covering casualties caused by the long distance shelling from the French side and vessels that grounded on the Goodwin Sands. Syd recalls that, if you did not get them off within 48 hours, they started to break up. At least the salvage ships found food and supplies on the damaged Liberty ships. Their counterparts on the French side were amazed to find that there was much more food in France than they were used to seeing; perhaps this was why many of the French were none too keen to be 'liberated.'

All crews remember the rough times clearing up on the casualties with the stink of cordite still around as they shovelled debris over the side; debris that included body parts. There was not even time to deal with the corpses properly. Some of the crew could not cope, but most were so weary that they 'accepted it'. Syd says how sorry he felt for the dead 'Yanks, floating around in their fancy uniforms', as he says, 'to come all that bloody way and to end up like that.'

Syd was the last man to leave his *Longtow* after VE Day. Then he was called to the Yard as he was wanted as Bosun on the *LC3*. This was a less than happy time; the barge was short of gear, much of it having been sold on the black market in Antwerp and the only lighting was by Tilley lamps. Syd went from Bosun to Mate and then became Skipper when the Master went sick. Most of their work was in and around Southampton Docks. Then, with everything running down, he was moved to the *American Salvor* as Bosun. He was later offered the Mate's job but turned it down; 'the job wasn't what it used to be'. He decided it was time to 'swallow the anchor' and get married.

Chester Vernon 'George' Major

George was launchman on a Coastal class waiting to go to the 'Far Shore'; he was sent ashore to Hillhead with the ration books to queue up and get what food he could. George was not too familiar with the waters at the Haven, he took a short cut and went ashore on a falling tide. It was only then, when the sky became full of aircraft and gliders, he realised that the great day had come. Sadly George did not record his part in the invasion.

George was the Second Engineer on the Risdon Beazley ship *Droxford*.

Thus, the biggest salvage effort in history came to a close. Obviously, there was much removal work to complete, but, without the efforts of Cyril, George, Peter, Syd, Tom and Tony and the many hundreds like them, the ports would have been unusable and the liberation would have ground to a halt.

If Risdon Beazley Ltd had not existed others would have risen to the occasion. But this does not alter the fact that these men and their company did take on the task and did everything that was asked of them.

But the men never fell into the trap of taking themselves too seriously; Tony ended his story with:

> During my time with the Salvage vessels someone had pinned up in the mess a quotation from Churchill that referred to "The heroic and marvellous feats of the Salvage Services" but we rather preferred the cartoon that one of the lads had drawn. This showed a cargo ship beset with all sorts of trouble, planes strafing it, subs torpedoing it, and mines floating all around and from its bridge to the Salvage ship steaming toward it, the signal "Go away – don't you see we've got enough trouble already!"

M.V. *Nezo*, Tommy Thomson, Normandy, 1944.

Tommy Thomson was a Shetland born seaman who kept good diaries of his time at sea. Bill Benson, also of Shetland, has provided about half of them and has obtained Tommy Thomson's family's permission to reproduce them.

After an adventurous time on his previous voyages, Thompson joined the Dutch Schuyt *Nezo* in London Docks on 22 May 1944, 15 days before the invasion of Europe. He remained on this little motor ship until the 8 August 1945, by which time the war in Europe was over.

I feel that his story needs no editing, though I have cut out an interesting account of a horse drawn cider press:

The Dutch coaster *Nezo*, 250 tons burden, registered in Delfzijl, was at Ipswich in the summer of 1944, where we had just finished discharging a cargo of coal, when we got orders to proceed to Southampton with all possible speed. The ship had been chartered by the United States Army, to ferry munitions ashore in Normandy from the ships lying at anchor in Seine Bay, and for which there was no port facilities. On our way up to Ipswich, and again on the way down the River Orwell, we passed a long line of invasion barges moored to buoys in the river. Painted grey with black and white camouflage and which looked like the real thing, until you got close to them, when their sides could be seen flapping in the wind. They were wood and canvas mock ups.

When we got to Southampton we were loaded with a cargo of ammunition for France, and a deck cargo of glass carboys in wicker baskets. We were told that they contained acid for spraying on the battlefields. We sailed from Southampton and were at anchor in the Solent for two days before joining a convoy for France. In the convoy was a tug towing a huge steel drum on which was painted the name HMS *Conundrum*.

We docked, at Cherbourg, which had just fallen to the Americans. There was a lot of damage apparent to the dock area, we were discharged here. Sailing from Cherbourg we went south along the coast to Seine Bay. It was full of an unimaginable amount of ships lying at anchor full of war material. This was to be our work for the next three months, helping to ferry their cargoes ashore.

The little port of Isigny on the River Aure had been taken by the American 175th infantry on the night of 8-9th June with little damage to the town. It lies a little less than a mile up the River Aure which flows into the Tire. This was to be our base. The *Nezo* had been taken for this work on account of her shallow draught, 8 feet, when loaded. The Aure was so narrow that on our first trips in there we had had to come out stern first, no room to turn around.

The Americans solved this problem with their usual efficiency. They set three bulldozers to work and carved a great half-moon out of the north bank of the Aure just below the town, sufficient to permit un-laden coasters to swing around.

Twelve Dutch coasters of our size were chartered by the American Army to operate out of Isigny, and a Capt Kramer was sent over here to act as shore Superintendent and to act as Liaison Officer with the Americans.

Although the town appeared to have escaped damage, everywhere in the surrounding fields were water filled bomb craters. Along the roads were white tapes with notices saying: "Mines Cleared to the Verges" and every here and there the evidence of it where holes had been dug to unearth the mines. In the fields dead unburied cattle lay which no one dared approach on account of mines. Everywhere were high hedges, beyond some of them were orchards and trees laden with apples, which no one dared go near. All of it had been mined.

From the multitude of ships lying off Utah Beach, vehicles were loaded on to landing- craft and thence landed on to the beaches. Low sandy foreshores with sand dunes built up at the back of the beaches, here and there bulldozers had cut gaps in the dunes. Vehicles coming off the landing craft could be seen going up the beach and disappearing through the gaps. They were also using amphibious craft called DUKW'S which would come off to the ships and load about two tons of cargo and head for the shore thence up the beach and through the gap in the dunes. Many of them were swamped on the way to the beach, I spoke with one black American driver of a DUKW who claimed to have had two of them sink under him.

Here in Isigny we ferried ashore every conceivable kind of gear needed by an army, bombs and shells, and all kinds of ammunition. Canvas engineering workshops and all the tools to go with them. All kinds of kitchen equipment; petrol, sometimes in four gallon Jerry cans, sometimes in forty gallon drums; fork lift trucks and baby tractors; Harley Davidson motor cycles and innumerable wooden cases containing spare parts for every kind of war machine; canvas field hospitals and all sorts of medical equipment to go with them; also landed were huge rolls of steel wire mesh for making air-strips.

On our first trips into Isigny the stevedores were American army personnel, sometimes black but not always. We came in one day with a full cargo of 45 gallon drums of petrol. An American soldier standing on the quay enquired, 'Is it gas all the way down' an unfamiliar term to us for petrol.

He then went on to ask about how the winch and the derrick and the guy-ropes operated. This was explained, he listened, and then he drawled 'You know I am the sea'. He was allocated the job of hauling on the guy rope, which swung the derrick ashore with its load of barrels. It was no time until he had purloined a baby tractor, which he hooked on to the guy rope, and sat there all day going back and fore, it was much quicker.

Later the discharging was often done by prisoners of war. The German prisoners which were sent down on board of us could hardly have been described as elite troops. A lot of them were old and some were very young, some looked no more than 16 or 17.

I tried to speak to one young German one day; he would probably have started his career in the Hitler Youth. He couldn't speak English, but he came away with a tirade against the Americans. 'American plane Prima, American tank Prima, American truck Prima, American nix Prima'.

They were not to be trusted too far. One day kitchen equipment was being discharged and the American guards caught them stealing kitchen knives.

The guards gave them short shrift, they were bundled straight ashore. It was always the same American Lieutenant who was in charge of the guards and the prisoners, so we got to know him well. He used to sit in the galley cum mess room and drink cups of coffee, and sometimes would play gin-rummy with us.

One day when we came in to discharge the prisoners were Russian instead of German. We were mystified as to how the Americans came to have Russians as prisoners, so we asked the Lieutenant how this could be. He explained that the Germans had captured them in Russia, and then coaxed them into joining the German Army. When the going got tough in the West they were sent there and were captured by the Americans. He also said "you know our interpreters have had a difficult time with them, trying to find out where they came from. Many are without education, and when asked where was their home, they would name the place, but when shown a map and asked to point where it was, they were unable to do so, the map meant nothing. This was further complicated by them coming from many different areas of Russia, and speaking many different dialects. Some of them didn't seem to know what it was all about, or who was fighting who.

Many of them were bearded venerable looking men, but there was a pathetic air of resignation about them, as though they had a sense of foreboding of what was in store for them. They were by far the best workers that we had in Isigny. At the end of the war there were 11000 of these Russian prisoners in camps in Britain. It is a sad reflection on our country that at the end of the war they were sent back to Russia to face mass execution by Stalin's firing squads. Some were sent to the Black Sea, and some to Murmansk. From the camps in Britain they were taken in blacked out trains to the seaports, so that they might not see any of the countryside.

On some dull and misty mornings, it was quite some job to locate the particular ship which we had been sent to among the multitude of vessels at anchor, and to avoid a collision. The only way it could be achieved was asking directions from whatever ship hove in sight. Sometimes this had to be repeated several times before finding the one we had been allocated. The stevedoring and off-loading of these ships at anchor all seemed to be done by black Americans, their Pioneer Corps, it was always them who stowed the cargo on board of us. They seemed to have all the skills of professional dockers in the handling of cargo, and they were spurred on with the urgency of getting the cargoes ashore as speedily as possible.

We needed high water to get into Isigny with a full cargo. The work continued around the clock, there was never any shortage of manpower at the discharging end. Prisoners were never used at night, or if we were landing a dangerous cargo. Sometimes for us sleep became a problem, and there were never many occasions when we had the chance of a walk ashore. One day Henry Gillen, the other AB, and I had been for a walk, and were on our way back, in the early afternoon, when we heard the noise of approaching vehicles.

It was an American armoured column coming over a bridge across the Aure, preceded by motorcycles. The street was so narrow that we came to be trapped in the recess of somebody's doorway, until the last vehicle had passed, which was over an hour later. The seemingly endless line of vehicles were huge tank transporters loaded with tanks, nose to tail, all new and shiny. The tailback must have extended for many miles. The street was just wide enough to take them, no room for anything else, not even a pedestrian.

They had come in from somewhere very muddy, as the treads of their monster tyres were loaded with mud, and when they had passed through, the normally clean street was now a river of mud many inches deep, and by which we were still trapped. The Americans had huge scraper blades mounted on bulldozers. One of these came down the street pushing a wall of mud which was decanted into the river. Soldiers cleaned up afterwards with hoses and water pumped from the river.

We seldom saw the town's people, they were swamped by the military presence. We did see a few motorcars which ran on producer gas, indicating that they had not seen petrol for a long time. One day we came in with a cargo of 500 lb bombs, each bomb was cradled in wood for transport, the Americans took away the bombs, but left the timber, which we dumped on the quay for anyone to have that wanted it, a considerable pile. There were plenty of locals in evidence then and pile of wood soon vanished.

The Americans lost a lot of men in the landing on Omaha, which beach became known as 'Bloody Omaha'. On a hillside not far away 3000 American boys lay buried.

Prior to the invasion of Europe the Allies had printed a vast amount of French francs, known as invasion francs, this was the currency used by the Allied armies in Normandy. If we asked for a sub on our wages it was in these that we were paid. Our mail from home came through the American army.

Theo De Boke, our Cook - Steward belonged to Antwerp, he was fluent in many languages, but especially in French & German & English. In his younger days he had been a chef in the Belgian Red Star liners running across the Atlantic.

The American army supplied our rations. Never any shortage in this respect, a great variety, even luxury items like ice cream and. canned fruit. Also there was what was known as PX rations, consisting of, cigarettes, sweets, chocolate, razor blades & toilet gear. Our Cook -

Steward would draw our rations weekly, from the Americans. PX rations were debited from our wages.

As the Allied armies progressed further and further eastward, so did the amount of ships coming into Seine Bay gradually taper off, and about the middle of November we were the only Dutch coaster left in Isigny. We too got orders to depart. We loaded some of the port installations, fork lift trucks, tractors and a small mobile crane and made our last trip out of Isigny. And the River Aure, with its little light beacon and its tide gauge at its junction with the Vire.

We were bound for Cherbourg where we arrived on the 20th November. We were a few days in Cherbourg, where we discharged our cargo and re loaded with ammunition. From there we went to Rouen, past the wrecked and blocked port of Le Havre, where we picked up a pilot to take us up the River Seine.

The Seine is narrow and winding with many acute bends, on one of those bends the retreating Germans had blocked the river by sinking two block-ships across it. Both were sitting on an even keel with their sterns towards the river banks. One of them was the Norwegian whale factory ship *Ole Wagger*, which the German raider *Pinguin* had captured in Antarctica, and which had been successfully brought to France with its valuable cargo of whale oil.

An American salvage team in conjunction with team from the Royal Navy had managed to swing the bows of the block-ships far enough apart to permit a coaster of our size to squeeze through (see the chapter on salvage). Whether or not we were the first ship up to Rouen is not known, but no other vessels were there when we arrived.

Tommy was the Ship's Carpenter on a number of Risdon Beazley salvage ships after the war.

Casualties

In retrospect, the number of merchant ship casualties during Neptune was mercifully small. As we saw in a previous chapter, the first loss was the *Sambut*, managed for the MOWT by 'Paddy' Henderson & Co. The ship had sailed from Southend at 0630 on 6 June in the 12 ship convoy ETM1. These British Liberty ships had been pre-loaded, with troops, their vehicles, equipment and stores, and large consignments of fuel and gelignite. The *Sambut* carried 562 troops and a crew of 63, including DEMS gunners.

This was the first convoy of deep-sea ships to transit the Dover Strait since the fall of France. All knew that they would be within the range of the shore batteries on the French side and hugged the English shore. Near noon on the 6 June, the *Sambut* was hit twice. The first shell struck abaft the engine room and the second close forward of the bridge. The fire-fighting equipment was wrecked and within ten minutes a fire was raging, particularly among the loaded vehicles on deck.

Soon the gelignite in a lorry on No 2 hatch detonated, wrecking the navigation bridge and the portside lifeboats. By then the fire was spreading rapidly and Captain Mark Wills ordered 'abandon ship'. Six of the crew had been killed. The rest got away in the starboard lifeboats, with the exception of the Master, Chief Officer and the sea pilot who remained to supervise the launching of the thirty rafts for the troops. Once these were in the water, they told the soldiers to jump in and board them. Many were 'diffident', but jumped when they were told that the ship could blow up at any moment. That morning Captain Wills had given instructions that all troops should wear lifebelts.

The Master, Chief Officer, and Pilot left the ship at 1240, when none of the living remained. They jumped over the side and swam to a raft, through a number of dead bodies. The Master believed that many of the other dead were on the troop deck, in the vicinity of the explosion.

The survivors were picked up by a number of vessels, including a Corvette and four motor launches from Dover. In his report the Master comments on the unsuitability of the MLs for rescue work, with their high sides and inexperienced crews. The *Sambut* continued to be rocked by explosions and the burning hulk was torpedoed by the Royal Navy, as it was a hazard to shipping.

The Personnel convoy ETP 1 was the next to transit the Dover Strait, fortunately without loss.

On 8 June 1944 the *Chant 61* capsized and sank off the Normandy beaches; she had brought petrol from Thameshaven. There is no record of crew losses. As these vessels have not been described elsewhere in the book, it may be appropriate to give a brief description here. During the planning process, it became obvious that it would be prudent to design a coastal tanker that could carry either bulk or cased petrol, at least until the PLUTO system came into operation. With the shipyards, working at full capacity it was decided that the 28 component parts of the ships should be built by inland fabricators and road hauled to the ship builders for assembly. This method had already been used for the TID tugs.

The ships were 148′ overall, with a beam of 27′. They were just over 400 grt and 450 dwt. Various diesel engines in the range 220/270 horse power were fitted, giving a service speed of about 7 ½ knots. The hulls were made up of flat plate, with a double chine (the corner at the bilge) and double skinned. Forty-three were built and a further 25 were completed as dry cargo coasters. The latter were initially called Fabrics; they went into service with Empire names, each beginning with F.

The result was not as ugly as it sounds, though they seem to have been somewhat unstable and were apparently a nightmare to steer. The *Chant 63* had capsized and sank off Flamborough Head on 5 June.

Chant 60 and *Chant 61*, **J Readhead and Sons, South Shields.**
Tyne and Wear Archives via Wikipedia.

Early in the morning of 10 June the US Liberty ship *Charles Morgan* was hit by a bomb in No 5 hold. The ship sank by the stern at the Utah inner anchorage.

On 11 June (Winser says the 10th) the 13 ship unescorted coastal convoy ETC 4W was attacked by an S-Boote flotilla, when about four hours from their destination. The ships of the convoy were loaded with petrol and ammunition. Two modern coasters, the diesel powered *Ashanti* (Evans Ltd) and the steamer *Brackenfield* (Savage Ltd) were attacked and sank quickly. They were followed by the World War One veteran *Dungrange,* (Buchan & Hogg Ltd), which had gone to the assistance of the *Brackenfield*. Thirty-three died, including the three Masters. Also on the 11th the, almost new, Admiralty tug *Sesame* sank following an explosion. The only two (three?) survivors found themselves in the water with no idea what had happened.

The British Tanker Co (BP) *British Engineer* was on passage to the Omaha beach with a cargo of petrol and diesel oil. At 2150 on 12 June, a mine exploded amidships. The ship was diverted to the Solent, where she transferred part of her cargo, before taking the balance back to Thameshaven.

On the 14 June the *Chant 69* capsized off the Normandy beaches, she was sunk by gunfire.

The Trinity House buoy tender *Alert* had been off the French coast since 7 June. On the 16[th,] she struck a mine while on passage from Gold to her base at Cowes. The ship was taken in tow, but sank shortly thereafter; none of the crew was lost. Trinity House received a letter from Admiral Sir Bertram Ramsay, expressing his appreciation for the excellent work the *Alert,* and her sisters, had carried out.

Convoy EBC 14 assembled off Barry on 17 June with cargo for Utah beach; it was comprised of eighteen ships, but no escorts. After dark on the evening of 18 June, aircraft were heard overhead, the ships in the convoy did not open fire as they were unable to ascertain if these were Allied planes. Just before midnight, the Canadian Laker *Albert C Field* was hit by an aerial torpedo; the ship broke in two and sank in four minutes. Four of the crew and one DEMS gunner died. As the lifeboats had been destroyed in the attack, the survivors escaped on the rafts. The *Albert C Field* was carrying 2,500 tons of ammunition and 1,300 bags of mail, which had been loaded in Penarth.

The next day the elements became the main enemy. The weather had improved considerable by the afternoon of the 7 June and better conditions continued through until the 14th, from then on it deteriorated. There was a brief improvement during the night of 17th - 18th, but this was 'the calm before the storm'. On the 19th a north easterly gale began, which did not cease until the 22nd. It has since become known as the 'Great Storm'; the worst in forty years according to some. Admiral Ramsay refers to 'The Northerly Gale'. The main problem was that it was not forecast and that it came from the worst possible direction, this, combined with low pressure, caused a storm surge. In all eight hundred items of wreckage were recorded, obviously a rounded figure.

The first merchantman to become a casualty of the storm was another of the Chants; this time *Chant 7*, which capsized and was driven ashore on the 19th. One source says that the little tanker was driven through a hedge and into a field. There were five merchant casualties on the 20 June. *Asa Eldridge*, one of the US built 'jeeps', was damaged after grounding on the Calvados shoal. The ship was re-floated the next day. When the tug *Cheerly* arrived in the Solent with the *Asa Eldridge,* the tow was found to need repairs to her steering gear and boilers, in addition to the bottom damage. Another coaster, the *Chelwood,* also went ashore on the same shoal; she spent two very uncomfortable days there before the salvage teams re-floated her. She was then taken into Mulberry B for discharge. The work load for the salvage teams was enormous; more on that later.

Chant 23 was beached during the gale, and was later towed back to Sheerness. The coaster *Rondo* sustained considerable damage when rammed by landing craft,; and the coaster *Citrine* struck an underwater object and was grounded until the 24th.

Ashore, the enemy guns were little affected by the gale and continued to make things very uncomfortable for the ships that were riding it out. The cargo ship *Derrycunihy* arrived off the Normandy coast on the 20th, on her third trip to the beaches. They were at the extreme eastern end of the Bridgehead, where they and others frequently came under fire from the shore batteries near Le Havre. The Master would have been on the bridge for several days, without a break. The first indication that they were a target would come when they heard the sound of a shell. This would fall on one side of the ship and the next shell would fall on the other side. The soldiers aboard knew that these were ranging shots. The Master would then move the ship with the main engines, but this was agonisingly slow. Once they completed the move, the whole nerve wracking attack would start again, unless the shore gunners had decided to target another ship. For the unfortunate *Derrycunihy,* and her troops, far worse was to come.

The gale continued through the 21st, but the only merchant casualty was Hay's *The President.* Though she that been built as recently as

1936 the only thing that was imposing about this coal-fired steam collier was her name. In fact, she was typical of so many of the British coasters. During the gale, conditions on these ships must have been most unpleasant, particularly for the firemen labouring in the boiler room; they knew that if their ship was hit their chances of survival were slim.

The gale eased on the 22nd and discharging resumed, though there was still a considerable sea running. Among the first to start unloading was the coaster *Wallace Rose*; she had lost both anchors in the storm and steamed off the lee shore for two days. The *Eilian Hill*, a steam coaster, was damaged at Port-en-Bessin.

Another coaster, the *Kylegorm*, ran aground at Gold. The salvage report is typically brief 'Attended & repaired by *Sea Salvor*. Refloated. Towed to the UK.' The salvors were then called to assist the *Dunvegan Head*; here the report says 'Ammunition ship shelled and burned out. Surveyed and considered a constructive total loss.' The TNA file ADM1/17274 contains many of these minimal reports. For some reason the *Dunvegan Head* was beached at Sword in an area that 'had already been closed to coasters.' The crew were ashore sheltering when the vessel was hit by two shells, which set the cargo ablaze. The fire was not extinguished until 24 June. Elsewhere there is a reference to an ammunition coaster being told to dock at Ouistreham, where the 80 AA Brigade was to provide cover. It is not known whether this was the same ship.

On the 23rd, there were a number of naval casualties, but only two merchant ships; these were the coasters *Avanville* and *Nestun*. The first was damaged and beached at Sword. The other was damaged by a mine, flooding a hold; she was beached and discharged at Omaha.

M V *Derrycunihy* was one of the versions of an Economy Doxford and was only four months old when she loaded for Normandy. She had had a bad time riding out the gale, while coming under fire.

M.V. "DERRYCUNIHY." Built for **McCowen & Gross Ltd., London.** Shelter Deck—Coal, Grain and General Cargo. Length b.p. 425'-0". Breadth 57'-0". Depth mld. 37'-9" to shelter deck. Deadweight—10,200 Tons. Draft—27'-4½". Engines—Doxford opposed piston two cycle Diesel. Auxiliaries—Steam driven. Boilers—Two, oil-fired. B.H.P.—2550. Speed—12 Knots.

 She carried 583 troops and their stores and equipment, including loaded vehicles on deck. She had a crew of 37, 23 gunners, two Air Observers and one Military Storekeeper. Her Master was Captain Harold Richardson; the following account is taken from his report, I have omitted the paragraph numbers.

> We weighed anchor from "Sword" Beach at 0730 on 24th June. Whilst manoeuvring the ship to the Southward in order to clear mines which I had been informed were to the N.N.E of us, at 0735 on the 24th, in a position on the 4 ¾ fathom patch, off "Sword" Beach , steering on a Southerly course with only steerage way on, there was a loud explosion as the vessel struck a mine. The weather was fine and sunny, with good visibilty; there was a slight sea and N.E. wind, Force 2/3.
>
> The explosion occurred underneath the ship, near the after end of No. 4 hold, causing the after part of the hull to split at the bulkhead between the engine room and No. 4 hold. Within 30 seconds the after end of the

ship submerged, but the fore end remained afloat, the two ends still being connected by the keel plates. A large column of water was thrown up through the hatches, all communication from the bridge to the engine room were put out of action, and No. 4 hatches were blown away. There was a slight leak in the engine room tunnel, but the engine room remained dry. A car stowed on No. 4 hatch caught fire, setting fire to some petrol stowed on deck, so we were unable to control the fire which rapidly spread along the starboard side of the ship.   The four lifeboats were undamaged. One was lowered into the water as a precautionary measure, and the remaing three were lowered halfway.

Immediately after the explosion several M.L.'s and a Salvage Boat closed the ship; the M.L.'s transferred all survivors the s.s "CAP TOURANE", and by 0800 everybody was clear of the ship. The Salvage Boats remanined alongside to fight the fire. (The *Cap Tourane* was also shelled during the day.)

Captain Richardson returned to the casuaty at 0900, by which time the salvage crews already had the fire under control. The Salvage Officer said that their next task was to save the vehicles, before they attempted to salvage the ship. To drive the cargo winches a steam pipe had been connected from one of the salvage vessels. Discharge was still going on when the Master and Chief Engineer left the ship at 1630. The salvage report reads: 'Back broken, after end sunk, fore end floating – 109 army vehicles and other material salvaged undamaged from the fore end, ship total loss.' No mention of the intense fire, nor the risk from other of these new oyster mines in the area or shelling. The fore-end was salvaged later.

Fifteen gunners, one Air Observer and nine of the crew lost their lives; even more critical was the loss of 183 troops, with another 120 injured. In his report Captain Richardson comments on the presence of mind of Donkeyman (Petty Officer) Nicholson, who saved the life of a DEMS Sergeant by pulling him across the split after deck to safety.

About half an hour before the *Derrycunihy* was mined HMS *Swift* broke in two after striking another mine; seventeen were killed. At 0805 the s.s. *Fort Norfolk* suffered the same fate; she had completed discharge and was returning to the assembly anchorage. Her engine and boiler rooms were wrecked and the seven crew on duty there died.

The other merchant casualties on the 24th were the *Empire Lough* and the *Gurden Gates;* both were in convoy ETC 17, which was engaged by the coastal guns in France. *Empire Lough*, a war built collier, was laden with 2,800 tons of cargo: one source says cased petrol for Gold, another ammunition and government cargo. The ship was set on fire and was beached off Folkestone, where she was declared a total loss. Two died, including the Master. *Gurden Gates*, one of the US built 'Jeeps', was damaged in the same action.

On the 26 June it was decided that the US Mulberry A was so damaged that it was abandoned. Some of the components were used to repair or strenghten the less affected Mulberry B, which later became kmown as Port Winston. There were no further merchant casualties until 28 June.

The Cross Channel Packet *Maid of Orleans*, and the other LSIs, had maintained a shuttle service with troop reinforcements. On the evening of 28 June, she was returning to the UK, when there was an explosion. It has never been established whether she struck a mine or was hit by a torpedo. Smoke and escaping steam, rose high in the air and the Maid rolled over and sank.

She had begun her career transporting troops to France in the final couple of months of the Great War. In 1940 she made six trips to Dunkirk,; being diverted once and in collision on the final trip. In the other four trips, she saved 5,503 troops; a record only bettered by the excursion ships *Royal Daffodil* (7,461), *Royal Sovereign* (6,370), and HMS *Malcolm* (5,991). Operation Dynamo is another operation where the Merchant Navy's valuable contribution has never been acknowledged. there are others.

The Maid's Red Ensign is laid up in St Earnsywth's Church at Folkestone. The plaque reads:

> The ensign of the cross channel steamer "Maid of Orleans" which struck a mine while returning from the Normandy beaches on June 28th 1944 and was presented to the church on June 28th, 1946 by Captain M L Payne OBE, RD in memory of his ship and of the five members of the crew who lost their lives.

Also on the 28 June, the US Liberty ship *Charles W Eliot* was mined and sunk, while moving to the assembly anchorage after discharging at Juno.

Four more ships were seriously damaged on the 29th. The British *Empire Portia* was mined; she was towed back to the Solent with a flooded engine room. While on passage to Utah beach the US flagged Liberty ships, *H G Blasdel*, *James A Farrell* and *John A Treutlen* were all torpedoed by *U 984*. *H G Blasdel* was towed back to the Solent for discharge, by the tug *Amsterdam*. The *James A Farrell* was also towed back to the Solent; firstly by the tug *Caldy* and then by the *Zwarte Zee*. The *John A Treutlen* returned to the Solent, this time behind the US tug *Farallon*. None of the Liberties were repaired.

The British declared the end of Operation Neptune on 30 June. Their American allies did so on 3 July, but not before one final loss: the *Empire Broadsword* was mined while returning from Omaha. She rolled over and sank at 1835 on the 2 July. It is said that seven lost their lives, though only two are commemorated at Tower Hill.

A glimpse of the storm damage in the US Sector   Source unknown

The salvage plan was to allocate a pair of self-propelled lifting craft to each of the two British beaches and another pair to the mainly Canadian beach, with the fourth as back-up. These were to start arriving at D+1. Ideally, they would have all been Coastal Class salvage ships but only five were in service by May 1944, and one of those was working in the Mediterranean. So each Coastal was paired with an older lifting craft. Each British beach also had one of the US built salvage ship and a Royal Navy wreck clearance vessel. There were a number of the non-propelled lifting craft, which were allocated as required. Five vessels were kept in reserve to begin the clearance of the captured ports. The salvage vessels each had a large S painted on the funnel.

At Omaha and Utah the US Navy vessels included *U.S.S Brant*, *U.S.S Diver* and *U.S.S Swivel* – sisters of the US built vessels serving under the British flag. After the mid-June storm the need for lifting craft at the Western Beaches became obvious. The British transferred the 'spare pair', *Help* and *Abigail,* to the U.S sector, together with four of the non-propelled lifting craft. American reports acknowledge how useful these vessels were to them; they continued to use them in Cherbourg and afterwards. The British crews enjoyed the American can-do attitude, and the superior rations!

Port-en-Bessin   © Crown Copyright: Courtesy Battlefield Historian

**Port-en-Bessin, 13 June 1944, *Lifeline*? See above.
Appears in publications as IWM, but cannot be traced by IWM.**

As has been said the salvage reports were brief and tell little of the tremendous work done by the salvage department. It is difficult to assess the extent of that work, but a total of 315 jobs were carried out at, and off, the British beaches in about three months. The awards give some idea of what was achieved:

Captain Geoffrey Storr, Master, s.v. *Lifeline*, D.S.C.
Captain Rieth Stonehouse Lennard, Master, s.v. *Help*, Civil O.B.E.
Captain James White, Master, s.v. *Abigail*, Civil O.B.E.

British Empire Medals:

Hugh Ross Allan, Diver, s.v. *Uplifter*.
Harry William Bentley, Boatswain, s.v. *Kingarth*.
John Gordon Smith, Senior Diver, s.v. *Help*

There were Commendations for:

William Gardner McPherson , Chief Engineer, s.v. *Abigail*
James Sangster Melville Craig, Carpenter & Diver, s.v. *Abigail*
William Charles Sidney Irons, Second Mate and Boatswain, s.v. *Help*
James McKenzie, Boatswain, s.v. *Abigail*

The following were Mentioned in Despatches:

Captain W G Dalton Master, s.v. *Foremost 18*
W Kirby, Boatswain, s.v *Foremost 18*
D Munson A.B. s.v. *Foremost 18*
J J Haliday, Diver s.v. *American Salvor*
W C Whiting, Chief Engineer s.v. *Lincoln Salvor*

Acting Temporary Lt. Cdr D J R Davies, RNR was recommended for a decoration for 'salvage operations on the Normandy beaches and port clearance in the US Sector'

To be an Additional Member of the Military Division of the Third Class, of the Most Honourable Order of Bath: Commodore Second Class Thomas McKenzie C.B.E. R.N.V.R. For distinguished service in organising, salvage operations in the liberated ports in the British Assault Area in France.
(He also worked jointly with the Americans at Cherbourg – R.V.M.)

For work on the British, coast during & after the Normandy Landings: Percy Harold Carrington, Salvage Officer, Risdon Beazley, an M.B.E.

Some have citations, others do not.

PLUTO

Among the greatest of the supply problems was how to get petrol (gas) across the Channel and on to the fighting units; in particular the Americans required it in vast quantities. The British were fortunate that they had been able to copy the German, hence 'jerry', cans. These were far superior to the cans that they had used until then; but handling vast numbers of these would have been near impossible.

 The alternative was bulk handling with tankers; but these were always in short supply and required quite sophisticated shore facilities, something they knew would probably not be left in operational condition at the Normandy ports. Also oil storage tanks could easily be set on fire with shells or by sabotage. The ships were susceptible to attack by U-boats, E-boats, aircraft and shelling.

It was decided that the best solution would be to lay pipelines from Britain to France; but, like the Mulberry harbours, no one had ever done this before. The project was codenamed PLUTO, which has been accepted as being an acronym for **P**ipe **L**ine **U**nder **T**he **O**cean. This may, or may not, be correct. There are no explanations for the other codenames that were used for shorter fuel pipes: TOMBOLA and AMATHEA – see Port-en-Bessin below.

The first prototype was based on submarine telephone cables that had been developed over many years; but without the conductors and insulation. Here the codename was HAIS, which stood for - **H**artley, **A**nglo **I**ranian, **S**iemens: in order – the head of development, the oil company he worked for and the manufacturers. When a test pipe was laid by a Post Office cable ship in the Thames Estuary it worked well, so an order was placed for a slightly larger version.

Other tests followed; then a pipe was laid across the Bristol Channel only seven months after the scheme had originally been proposed. This was done by an especially modified ship HMS *Holdfast*, the former Dundee Perth and London Shipping Company's *London*. The *Holdfast* could carry and lay thirty miles of HAIS cable. Ellerman's *Algerian* was similarly modified. Neither vessel could lay a single run of pipe from Britain to France, so two standard MOWT tramp ships were also converted. The *Empire Ridley* became HMS *Latimer* and the *Empire Baffin* the HMS *Sancroft*; both could handle 100 miles of pipe. In their time, they were the two largest vessels of their type in the world. Two motor barges were modified to land the shore ends and various other small craft were requisitioned.

The reader might wonder what this has to do with Merchantmen at Normandy; it is that the crews of these vessels had almost all been merchant seamen.

The next problem was that there was not enough lead available to manufacture the pipe needed. This problem was solved with the design and manufacture of a flexible steel pipe. For this design, the Iraq and Burmah oil companies were approached. This pipe was named HAMEL after their chief engineers H A Hammick and B J Ellis. The less flexible steel pipe required a larger drum size than even the bigger ships could mount; so an enormous floating drum was designed, which had cone at one end. This became the Conun drum, or Conundrum.

Two HAIS and two HAMEL pipes were laid across the Channel in August, the first by HMS *Latimer* in only ten hours. The project was not without its problems and it was not until 22 September that pumping began. Even then, the flow rates were less than had been hoped.

This meant that tankers were still needed to carry fuel across the Channel and many cargo ships were also loaded with petrol in jerry cans. Four ship-to-shore pipelines were laid off Port-en- Bessin. These were in operation by the 24 June and could handle six hundred tons per hour, though they seldom achieved that throughput.

The PLUTO system came into its own later, when eleven HAIS and six HAMEL lines were laid from Dungeness to Boulogne. These were soon pumping up to one million gallons of fuel per day.

The Aftermath

In his 'covering letter' to his report on Operation Neptune Admiral Ramsay said:

> Because, in the event, the movements of over 5,000 ships and craft proceeded smoothly, and to plan, and because, despite bad weather, the Allied armies and air forces were landed and reinforced, if not as quickly as the optimum planning figure, at least more quickly than the enemy reinforced his forces by land, it may now appear that the size and complexity of the naval problem was somewhat exaggerated. This was not the case. That the operation proceeded smoothly and according to plan was the result of the hard work and foresight of the many thousands concerned in its preparation and the determination and courage of tens of thousands of Allied navies and merchant fleets who carried out their orders in accordance with the very highest traditions of the sea.

At the end of Operation Neptune on 30 June, the Royal Navy started requisitioning the Empire Class Infantry Landing ships; the first was the *Empire Arquebus*. No reason has been given for this transfer. It is more likely that, no longer having to man the LCTs (Tank Landing Craft), the Navy now had a surplus of men.

From November, they began renaming them, after Derby race winners. Three were not transferred: the *Empire Broadsword*, which was sunk on 2 July 1944, the *Empire Javelin*, which was sunk on 28 December 1944 and the *Empire Rapier*. The first two sank after explosions; it is not clear whether these were caused by mines or torpedoes. Several were sent to South East Asia, but they were not needed as the Japanese 'faded away'.

MOWT Name	RN Name	Pennant	
Empire Anvil	HMS Rocksand	F184	
Empire Arquebus	HMS Cicero	F170	Transferred end June

Empire Battleaxe   HMS Donavon   F161

Empire Broadsword   Mined and sank 2 7 1944

Empire Crossbow   HMS Sainfoin   F183

Empire Cutlass   HMS Sansovino   F162   Mined 21 11 1944 repaired

Empire Gauntlet   HMS Sefton   F123

Empire Halberd   HMS Silvio   F160

Empire Javelin   Sunk by U-Boat 28 12 1944

Empire Lance   HMS Sir Hugo   ?

Empire Mace   HMS Galtee More   F171

Empire Rapier

Empire Spearhead

Only two instances of 'under performance' have been found. One was an occasion on an exercise in Lyme Bay, when the troops returned to an LSI after the ship's crew had sat down to their evening meal. The deck crew were told to leave their food in order to recover the LCAs, which they declined to do. The situation was further aggravated by them being told that they would not get an overtime payment.

Later one of the Convoy Commodores complained that, despite an agreement with the unions and the MWOT, a ship's crew insisted that their lifeboats should be returned. It is not clear why they had been taken off in the first place, as the ships were arranged so that the lifeboats were clear of the LSA launching areas. The ship concerned was not even in the Commodore's convoy!

The merchant ships in the invasion fleet can be distinguished by having the prefixes m.v. (motor vessel) and s.s (steamship), rather than HMS or USS.

After the war many of those who had joined the Merchant Navy during the conflict received a nasty shock; they were told that, unless they had completed a minimum period at sea (four years?), they were liable to do National Service. This usually meant two years 'square bashing' in the Army. The British Legion regarded them as 'non-combatants'.

For whatever reason the service provided by civilians, both in the Merchant Service and elsewhere, has largely been forgotten. It is not possible to determine whether this is intentional.

Great Britain, which, at the start of the war, had the largest merchant fleet in the world, has not preserved even one of its deep sea ships. The American's keep two Liberty ships in commission and two, or more, Victory ships. They presented the last of the Liberties to Greece. Most other nations have kept representative merchant vessels, depending on their own specialities; for instance, the Dutch are particularly keen retaining tugs.

As Rose George says in her book Deep Sea and Foreign Going: 'The last time the Merchant Navy was thought to be heroic was 70 years ago, and its limelight was brief, like the sun breaking through the clouds then gone again.'

In a sub-title to the fifth volume of his History of the Merchant Navy Richard Woodman calls the demise of our merchant fleet 'The Great Squandering'. He is right to do so. Now our politicians are talking about making Britain 'a great trading nation again', but how can we do this without our own Merchant Service? What should be even more concerning is that we no longer have this essential lifeline should there be another war. This time we really could have our 'neck wrung like a chicken' as the French put it in 1940 and a new Churchill, if we find one, will not be able to say 'Some Chicken, Some Neck'.

Postscript

My first reliable memories are of the farm that my father had been brought up on, with the interesting name of Hollow Ditch. His father had been killed in the First World War. His mother died some years later, of TB or a broken heart, depending which family tale you believe. Her younger sister had taken him on, a solitary life for a lad.

I spent some of my school holidays on the farm. The memories I have date from 1942/3, by which time my uncle had died and my aunt was just keeping enough stock to meet her needs, including a single lonely cow.

In December 1943 my great aunt was one of the hundreds who were told to vacate their homes as the area was needed by the army for 'training'. We now know that this training was for D-Day. Many readers will have heard of the 'lost village' of Tyneham, but may not be aware of the larger area requisitioned at the same time. The tenants were promised that they could return when the war was won; but of course, they never did.

Hollow Ditch, 1943 and 2010

The 1943 photograph one of a series taken by Sgt Bert Hardy for the US Army. I have pasted a picture of the old couple in their porch, though Uncle Mat had died in 1939. My wife and I are the couple in the 2010 picture.

The Army still control that part of Purbeck, though they do not seem to use the area around Hollow Ditch for live firing. When I enquired about visiting the farm, and the hamlet of Whiteway where a great, great, grandfather built a cottage in the 1830s, the military were most helpful. For me it is interesting, but rather sad, to compare the photographs with the 'then and now' photographs of Normandy.

On 2 June 1944 we were near Weymouth and were amazed to see the seemingly endless columns of US vehicles making for the port. Some of these troops, many of them African Americans, would have lost their lives on the beaches of 'Bloody Omaha'.

My D-Day memory is of being at home, near the Royal Tank Corp's base at Bovington, looking up at a sky full of planes towing gliders.

Bibliography

Operation Neptune

The D-Day Ships, Neptune: the Greatest Amphibious Operation in History, John de S Winser

Operation Neptune, Kenneth Edwards

en.wikipedia.org/wiki/Operation Neptune

Chapter 2: Planning and Preparation

http://www.da.mod.uk/colleges/jscsc/jscsc-library/archives/operation-overlord

http://www.naval-history.net/WW2CampaignsNormandy.htm

www.history.navy.mil/library/online/comnaveu/comnaveu_index.htm

en.wikipedia.org/wiki/List_of_Allied_warships_in_the_Normandy_landings

http://www.physicstoday.org/resource/1/phtoad/v64/i9/p35_s1?bypassSSO=1 Tides

Working up

http://www.history.army.mil/documents/WWII/beaches/bchs-7.htm

Crew

A History of the British Merchant Navy, Volume Five Fiddler's Green, The Great Squandering: 1921-2010. Richard Woodman ISBN 9780752448220.

Le Maritime Regiment Royal Artillery, 1939-1945. Robert Le Chantoux. Militaria, No. 381, Juin 2017

Salvage Vessels

Admiralty Coastal Salvage Vessels, Design and Service 1943 – 1993. David Sowdon ISBN 0954331044. Also his articles in World Ship Society publications.

Risdon Beazley, Marine Salvor. Roy Martin and Lyle Craigie-Halkett. Amazon

The Battle for the East Coast' by J P Foynes. Published privately.

Assault Ships

Michel Sabarly assault group S3

http://ww2talk.com/forums/topic/38764-sword-beach/page-3?hl=sword

ADM 101/655 Elissa (RN Base Messina) Empire Javelin. Closed for 84 years from 1944(why?). May be someone will read this when I'm gone?

Cargo Ships

Liberty ships. Workhorse of the Fleet by Gus Bourneuf Jr. Published by ABS. www.scribd.com/doc/91635896/Workhorse-of-the-Fleet.

Mulberry

MCHS 0124.02.01 - The Mulberry Harbours. The Mulberry Harbours - My Final Assessment by Brigadier A E M Walter CBE

http://www.combinedops.com

Final Assessment

D-Day Files/Overlord files for Brigadier A E M Walter's 'Final Assessment

Operation Neptune report submitted to the Supreme Commander, Allied Expeditionary Force on the 16th October, 1944, by Admiral Sir Bertram H. Ramsay, K.C.B., M.V.O., Allied Naval Commander-in-Chief, Expeditionary Force. Supplement to the London Gazette, 28 October 1947.

The Aftermath

Written Evidence to the UK Transport Select Committee MGS0001, Roy Martin

Ships involved

No.	Coasters		No.	

No.	Coasters
1	AARO
	ABILITY
3	ACTINIA
4	ACTIVITY
11	ALACRITY
14	ALUEN GIFFORD
	ALBERT C FIELD
RD413	ALCOYNE
18	ALGOL
20	ALNWICK
RD405	AMAZONE
25	ANDONI
33	ANTICOSTI
US	ANTILOPE
35	ANTIQUITY
36	ANTHONY ENRIGHT
37	ANTRIM COAST
38	APRICITY
	ARA
41	ARBROATH
NS	ARDGANTOCK
43	ARDGRYFE
46	ARIDITY
48	ASA ELRIDGE
49	ASEITY
50	ASHANTI
51	ASBEL HUBBARD
53	ASHMUN J CLOUGH
54	ASK
56	ASSIDUITY
59	ASTERIA
62	ATLANTIC COAST
67	AVANCE
68	AVANCE 1
69	AVANVILLE
NS	AXINITE
72	BAILEY FOSTER
	BALDUIN
NS	BALTEAKO
NS	BEDENHAM
	BARONSCOURT
84	BEAL
85	BEECHFIELD
86	BEESTON
87	BELFORD
	BELLATRIX
92	BENJAMIN SHERBURN
93	BENGUELA
100	BERRYDEN
103	BIDASSOA
104	BIRKER FORCE
107	BLACKTOFT

233	CYRUS SEARS
RD406	DA COSTA
235	DAGENHAM
238	DALEWOOD
240	DAWLISH
242	DEERMOUNT
244	DEHBIGH COAST
US	DELFZIJL
253	DICKY
RD407	DOGGERSBANK
257	DONA FLORA
NS	DONAGHMORE
262	DORRIEN ROSE
264	DOWNLEAZE
265	DOWNSHIRE
266	DRAKE
US	DRITTURA
270	DUNGRANGE
RD408	DOURSWOLD
274	DUNVEGAN HEAD
276	DURWARD
282	EAGLESCLIFFE HALL
279	EAST COASTER
281	EASTWOOD
283	EBRIX
284	EDENSIDE
286	EDINA
287	EDLE
289	EGEE
294	EILDON
292	EILIAN HILL
295	ELIDIR
293	ELKANAH CROWELL
NS	EMERALD QUEEN
302	EMPIRE BANK
	EMPIRE BOND
303	EMPIRE CAPE
306	EMPIRE CLIFF
310	EMPIRE DAFFODIL
	EMPIRE CREEK
312	EMPIRE ESTUARY
314	EMPIRE FORELAND
317	EMPIRE HEARTH
322	EMPIRE JONQUIL
324	EMPIRE LAGOON
299	EMPIRE LEECH
326	EMPIRE LOUGH
327	EMPIRE NESS
328	EMPIRE NUTFIELD
3??	EMPIRE RESISTANCE
335	EMPIRE RIDER
333	EMPIRE SCOUT
	EMPIRE SEAMAN
334	EMPIRE SEDGE

336?	EMPIRE SHOAL	393	GIRONDE
NS	EMPIRE SNOWDROP (ex Caribe Du)	394	GLADONIA
338	EMPIRE STRAIT	396	GLAMIS
342	ENID MARY	397	GLANTON
345	ERIKA	399	GLEN
344	ERNA	401	GLEN GAIRN
346	ESKWOOD	402	GLEN DINNING
	EUTERPE	403	GLENGARRIFF
349	EVERTSON	1052	GOLDFINCH
	EXPRESS	412	GRANBY
353	FAGERBRO	413	GRANFOSS
355	FANO	414	GRANGETOFT
NS	FENDRIS	415	GRASLIN
358	FENJA	418	GRENAA
RD409	FICUCIA	419	GRETA FORCE
366	FIRE QUEEN	420	GREYFRIARS
369	FLATHOUSE	1053	GUDRUN MAERSK
372	FLUOR	426	GUERNSEY QUEEN
376	FOLDA	428	GUN
377	FORELAND	429	GURDEN GATES
379	FREEMAN HATCH	430	GWENTHILLS
383	FYLLA	431	HAARLEM
384	GALACUM	433	HALO
387	GARESFIELD	439	HARPTREE COMBE
388	GASTON MICARD	440	HAWARDEN BRIDGE
389	GATESHEAD	443	HEIEN
391	GEM	444	HEIIRE

445	HELDER	497	JOEFFRE ROSE
446	HELMOND	499	JOHN W. ARE/?
US	HELVETIA	RD411	JOLA
449	HENRI GERLINGER	504	JOSEWYN
451	HERBERT W. WALKER	505	JOSIAH P. CRESSEY
RD410	HERON	507	JULIA
455	HETTON	?	JUNE
456	HIGHWEAR	US	JUPITER
458	HILDUR 1	510	JUSTIN DOANE (DEANE)
461	HOLBORN HEAD	511	JUTA
US	HONDSRUG	514	KAIDA
467	HOVE	515	KALEV
US	INSP. MELLEMA	517	KATOWICE
472	IPSWICH TRADER	518	KATWIJK
475	ISAC	519	KENRIX
476	ISBJORN	520	KENTISH COAST
495	J.F.V.	521	KEYNOR
US	JACOBA	524	KIMBALL HARLOW
482	JADE	525	KMICIC
483	JAN BRONS	531	KNOWLTON
485	JARGOON	532?	KOLSDAL
490	JELLICOE ROSE	533	KONGSHAVEN
491	JERNFJELD	535	KORDECKI
492	JERNLAND	536	KRAKOW
494	JESSE G. COTTING	538	KUL (530?)
495	J F V	540	KYLE BANK
496	JIM	544	KYLE CASTLE

546	KYLE QUEEN	?	MARIE-FLORE
547	KYLE GORM	624	MARSDEN
548	KYLOE	625	MARKSWORTH
551	LABAN HOWES	628	MARX
555	LADY THOMAS	631	MAURICE ROSE
560	LAMBTONIAN	?	MELISSA
561	LARCHFIELD	635	MELITO
?	LEKA	657	MR. THERM
571	LEOVILLE	643	MOELFRE ROSE
579	LILIAN 1	642	MONKSTONE
580	LILLEAA	645	MONKSVILLE
584	LOANDA	647	MOORLANDS
583	LOCREE?	652	MOSES GAY
592	LOTTIE R	RD412	MULAN
594	LOWESTOFT TRADER	659	MUNIN
600	LYSAKER V	662	NARCCZ
601	LYSLAND	663	NATO
603	MACVILLE	665	NAVIEDALE
605	MAJORCA	670	NEPHRITE
609	MAKEFJELL	671	NESTTUN
607	MAMMY	US	NEZO
610	MAPLEFIELD	672	NEWLANDS
612	MARCEL	676	NIVERNAIS
614	MARGA	675	NJORD
616	MARI	682	NORMANDY COAST
618	MARIANNE II	685	NORTHGATE
?	MARIE	686	NUGGET

689	OBSIDIAN	771	REGFOS
688	OCEAN COAST	769	REIAS
692	OLEV	773	REUBEN SNOW
696	ORANMORE	NS	RIBBLEBANK
700	ORIOLE	775	RICHARD BEARSE
704	ORTOLAN	778	RINGEN
708	OOSTERHAVEN	786	ROCKLEAZE
711	OXFORD	787	ROCKVILLE
RD414	PACIFIC	784	RODNEY BAXTER
	PALACIO	792	RONAN
715	PAMELA	793	RONDO
719	PARKNASILLA	796	ROSE MARIE
720	PARKWOOD	801	ROWANFIELD
721	PAUL EMILE JAVARY	802	ROYAL
723	PEBBLE	804	RUNNELSTONE
736	PLASMA	807	SAINT ANGUS
740	POLGLEN	809	SAINT BEDAN
739	POLLY M	812	SAINT RULE
744	PORTHREPTA	815	SAMBRE
745	PORTIA	817	SAMUEL VERY
747	POZNAN	821	SANDHILL
748	PRASE	823	SARD
1054	PRINCE DE LIEGE	824	SARNIA
NS	PROCRIS	826	SCHELDT
759	QUENTIN	830	SEAVILLE
762	RAFTSUN	832	SEDULITY
767	REDCAR	836	SERENITY

841	SHERWOOD	910	SUMMITY
842	SIAK	415	SURTE RD?
843	SIGNALITY	922	TEESWOOD
850	SKARV		THE BARON
851	SKELWITH FORCE	928	THE EARL
854	SKUM	931	THE PRESIDENT
856	SLEMISH	932	THE VICEROY
857	S.N.A.8	936	THESEUS
858	S.N.A.10	938	THORE HAFTE
867	SOBORG	939	THORN (withdrawn!)
863	SODALITY	940	THORNABY
865	SOJOURNER	943	THYRA III
871	SOLLUND	RD416	TILLY
873	SOUTHPORT	948	TOMSK
874	SOUTHWICK	?	TON S
880	SPES	951	TOPAZ
US	SPARTA	953	TORFINN JARL
881	SPHENE	954	TORQUAY
883	SPIRALITY	958	TRES
854	STADION II	961	TROMP
880	SPES	964	TUDOR QUEEN
891	SAINT-ENOGAT	965	TULLY CROSBY
895	STALEY BRIDGE	972	ULSTER HERO
898	STANLEY FORCE	976	VALBORG
899	STANVILLE	977	VAN BRAKEL
900	STARKENBORG		VAREGG
906	STUART QUEEN	982	VESTMANROD

986	VILK	1035	YEWPARK
988	VLIESTROOM	1036	YEWTREE
990	VULCANUS		YOKEFLEET
992	WALDO HILL	1044	ZEELAND
993	WALENBURGH	1046	ZELO (1048?)
994	WALLACE ROSE	1049	ZUIDERHAVEN
995	WATERGATE	1050	ZUIDLAND
996	WATSON FERRIS	1051	ZUIJDERBURGH
US	WEGRO		
US	WESTERHAVEN		

Additional numbers allocated later

1001	WESTBURN	1058	BRITISH COAST
1002	WESTCLFFE HALL	1059	EMPIRE FACTOR (Chant 29)
1004	WESTDALE	1060	EMPIRE FABRIC (Chant 14)
1006	WESTLAND	NS =	Naval Stores ships

Colliers

1007	WESTON		ARY LENSEN
1008	WESTOWN		BARON RUTHVEN
1009	WHEATCROP		BILTON
1013	WILD ROSE		COLWITH FORCE
1023	WILLIAM BURSLEY		EMPIRE BOSWELL
1017	WILLIAM H. DANIELS		FELSPAR
1019	WILLIAM HOMAN		KYLE BUTE
1018	WILLIAM HOWLAND		METHILHILL
1022	WILNO		SINCERITY
1026	WINONA		THE DUKE
1027	WOOLER		TOLSTA HEAD

Coastal Tankers

1032	YEWGLEN		
1034	YEWMOUNT	Tank	BEN ROBINSON

Tank	BRITISH SCOUT
Chant	1, 2, 3, 4, 6, 7, 22, 23, 24 25,
Chant	26, 32, 42, 43, 44, 45, 50, 57,
Chant	55 ,59, 58,60,61,62,64,67,69
Tank	DARST CREEK
Tank	EMPIRE ALDERNEY
Tank	EMPIRE AUDREY
Tank	EMPIRE CADET
Tank	EMPIRE COAST
Tank	EMPIRE CRICKETER
Tank	EMPIRE DWELLER
Tank	EMPIRE GYPSY
Tank	EMPIRE HOMESTEAD
Tank	EMPIRE SETTLER
Tank	EMPIRE TROTWOOD
Tank	EMPIRE WRESTLER
Tank	GOLDEN MEADOW
Tank	HASTINGS
Tank	HEYSER
Tank	JUSTINE C ALLEN
Tank	LOMA NOVIA
Tank	LULING
Tank	PASS OF BALLATER
Tank	RIO BRAVO
Tank	ROUSEVILLE
Tank	SALT FLAT
Tank	SAXET

Tank	SEVEN SISTERS
Tank	SULPHUR BLUFF
Tank	WALNUT BEND
Tank	Y23 , 25, 28, 40 & 41
UK	**Salvage Vessels**
S44	AMERICAN SALVOR
A	BOSTON SALVOR
S48	LINCOLN SALVOR
S49	SOUTHAMPTON SALVOR.
S50	HELP
S59	LIFELINE
S61	SUCCOUR
S62	UPLIFTER
S67	ABIGAIL
S66	FOREMOST 17
S5	FOREMOST 18
S7	GALLIONS REACH
S9	LADY SOUTHBOROUGH
S76	LE LUTTEUR
LC	2, 14, 15, 17, 19, 2 0, 21, 22
S1	ALITA
S3	CARMENITA
S41	DORITA
S23	PALMSTON
S24	POLITA
S20	MISS ELAINE
S68	BERTHA

S?	FORDE		**Rescue Tugs**
S65	SALVAGE CHIEFTAIN		**AMSTERDAM (Du)**
S64	SALVEDA		**ARIKARA**
	SALVICTOR		**BANNOCK**
S51	SEA SALVOR		**JAUNTY**
Pump	BARENSZ (Du schuyt)		**KIOWA**
S4	DAPPER (Pump)		**MASTODONTE**
S47	DORIA (Pump)		**PINTO**
S46	EMPIRE DEMON (Pump)		**SCHELDE (Du)**
Pump	KING LEAR		**THAMES**
Pump	LAMB		**ZWARTE ZEE (Du)**
S18	LONGTOW (Pump)	W105	**GROWLER**
Pump	MIES (Du Schuyt)	W23	**SAMSONIA**
Pump	NOORD-STAD (Du schuyt)		**Other 'British' Tugs**
Pump	RICHARD II		ABEILLE 20
Acc.	ROEBUCK (pump)		ABEILLE 21
S27	ROSELYNE (pump)	W50	**ALLEGIANCE**
Acc.	SAMBUR (pump)	W141	**ANTIC**
Pump	SWIFT		ARCADIA
Pump	THAMES COAST	??	ARROMANCHES
Pump	TORDENSKJOLD (Nor.)		ASSIDUOUS
Pump	URMAJO	W68	**ATTENTIF**
Pump	VIDA (Du schuyt)		BADIA
S45	WATERCOCK (pump)	W69	**BANDIT**
Pump	YEWDALE (collier)		BAT
Pump	ZEEHOND	W49	**BUCCANEER**
Pump	ZEUS	W35	**CHAMPION**

W74	**SABINE**		**13-31**	**See US list**
W27	**ST MARTIN**		32	FORT ST CROIX
W81	**ST MELLONS**		33	FORT BILOXI
W131	**SAUCY**		34	FORT WALLACE
W125	**SEA GIANT**		35	FORT CREVECOEUR
W44	**SEAMAN**		36	FORT DEARBORN
W144	**SESAME**		37	FORT KASKASKIA
	SIMLA		38	BRADFORD CITY
	STOKE		39	COMBE HILL
	SUNSHINE		40	DEMERTON
W87	**STORMKING**		41	DERRYCUNIHY
	VINCIA		42	EMPIRE BRUTUS
	WATERCOCK		43	EMPIRE CALL

Bold RN tugs with pennant numbers

MT	**Military Transports**		44	EMPIRE CANYON
1	SAMPEP		45	EMPIRE CAPULET
2	SAMBUT		46	EMPIRE CELIA
3	SAMARK		47	EMPIRE DEED
4	SAMPHILL		48	EMPIRE DUKE
5	SAMZONA		49	EMPIRE EARL
6	SAMAROVSK		50	EMPIRE FALSTAFF
7	SAMDEL		51	EMPIRE FARMER
8	SAMNEVA		52	EMPIRE GENERAL
9	SAMOS		53	EMPIRE GLADSTONE
10	SAMINVER		54	EMPIRE GREY
11	SAMMONT		55	EMPIRE HEYWOOD
12	SAMVERN		56	EMPIRE LANKESTER
			57	EMPIRE NEWTON

58	EMPIRE PICKWICK	79	FORT RAE
59	EMPIRE PITT	80	FORT RELIANCE
60	EMPIRE PLOUGHMAN	81	FORT ROMAINE
61	EMPIRE PORTIA	82	FORT SLAVE
62	EMPIRE RHODES	83	FORT TREMBLANT
63	EMPIRE STUART	84	FORT WRIGLEY
64	FORT ASSINIBOINE	85	FORT YALE
	FORT AUGUSTUS	86	HOUSTON CITY
	FORT CHIPEWYAN	88	INDIAN CITY
	FORT LAC LA RONGE	90	SAMNESSE
	FORT ORANGE	91	LAMBROOK
	FORT TICONDEROGA	92	LLOYDCREST
	FORT YUKON	93	MALAYAN PRINCE
65	FORT BEDFORD	94	MARWARRI
66	FORT BRUNSWICK	95	OCEAN ANGEL
67	FORT CHARNISAY	96	OCEAN COURIER
68	FORT ESPERANCE	97	OCEAN STRENGTH
69	FORT FINLAY	98	OCEAN VAGRANT
70	FORT FORK	99	OCEAN VENGEANCE
71	FORT GIBRALTAR	100	OCEAN VIGIL
72	FORT HENLEY	101	OCEAN VIGOUR
73	FORT LIVINGSTONE	102	OCEAN VISION
74	FORT MCMURRAY	103	OCEAN VISTA
75	FORT MCPHERSON	104	OCEAN VOLGA
76	FORT NORFOLK	105	SAMYORK
77	FORT PIC	107	SAMSIP
78	FORT POLAR	108	STANRIDGE

109	TREVIDER		LSIL	CLAN LAMONT
110	VANCOUVER CITY		PP3	DEVONSHIRE
	ANGLO INDIAN		LSIH	DUKE OF ARGYLL
	DUNKELD		LSIH	**DUKE of WELLINGTON**
	EMPIRE DARING		LSIL	EMPIRE ANVIL
	EMPIRE MANDARIN		LSIL	EMPIRE ARQUEBUS
	EMPIRE PERDITA		LSIL	EMPIRE BATTLEAXE
	GREENWICH		LSIL	EMPIRE BROADSWORD
	MONKLEIGH		LSIL	EMPIRE CROSSBOW
	IMPERIAL VALLEY		LSIL	EMPIRE CUTLASS
	LANGLEECRAG		LSIL	EMPIRE GAUNTLET
	ORMINSTER		LSIL	EMPIRE HALBERD
	REMBRANDT (Du)		LSIL	EMPIRE JAVELIN
	RICHMOND HILL		LSIL	EMPIRE LANCE
	ROMNEY		LSIL	EMPIRE MACE
	WELSH TRADER		LSIL	EMPIRE RAPIER
	SAMHOLT		LSIL	EMPIRE SPEARHEAD
134	EMPIRE CHARMAIN (Heavy Lift v/l)		LSIL	**GLENEARN**

Landing ships & troopships

			LSIL	**GLENROY**
LSIH	AMSTERDAM		LSIH	**INVICTA**
LSIH	BEN-MY-CHREE		LSIH	ISLE OF GUERNSEY
LSIH	BIARRITZ		LSIH	ISLE OF THANET
LSIH	**BRIGADIER**		LSIH	LADY OF MANN
TRP	CAMERONIA		LSIH	LAIRDS ISLE
LSIH	CANTERBURY		PP4	LANCASHIRE
TRP	CHESHIRE		PP7	LEOPOLDVILLE (Be)
TRP	CITY OF CANTERBURY		LSIL	LLANGIBBY CASTLE

TRP	LONGFORD
TRP	LOUTH
LSIH	MAID OF ORLEANS
LSIH	MECKLEBURG (Dutch)
LSIL	MONOWAI (NZ)
TRP	NEURALIA
LSIL	PAMPAS (later **PERSIMMON**)
LSIL	**PRINCE BAUDOUIN**
LSIS	**PRINCE CHARLES (Bel)**
LSIM	**PRINCE DAVID (Can)**
LSIM	**PRINCE HENRY (Can)**
LSIS	**PRINCE LEOPOLD (Bel)**
LSIH	PRINCESS MARGARET
LSIH	PRINCESS MAUD
LSIS	**PRINS ALBERT (Bel)**
LSIS	**PRINSES ASTRID (Bel)**
LSIS	**PRINSES J CHARLOTTE (Bel)**
LSIM	**QUEEN EMMA (Dutch)**
LSIH	**ST HELIER**
LSIH	**ULSTER MONARCH**
LSIH	VICTORIA
PP6	WORCESTERSHIRE

Tankers

Tank	BRITISH ENGINEER
Tank	BRITISH PRINCESS
Tank	BRITISH RENOWN
Tank	BRITISH STATESMAN

Tank	DOLABELLA
Tank	EMPIRE FLINT
Tank	EMPIRE PYM
Tank	EMPIRE RUSSELL
Tank	EMPIRE TRAVELLER
Tank	GOLDSHELL
Tank	JULIANA
Tank	LUCITA (Du)
Tank	**RAPIDOL**
Tank	SAN UBALDO

Accommodation Ships

Acc	AORANGI
Acc	ASCANIUS
Acc	CAP TOURANE
Acc	THYSVILLE
Acc	TORDEN SKJORD

Mooring Vessels, all HMS?

Netlayer	ATLANTA (Blackpool)
Netlayer	BRITTANY (Southern Railway)
Carrier	CAVEROCK (Verano, Gibraltar)
Depot	FERMOOR (Runciman)
Depot	FOSS BECK (C Lensen)
Carrier	KIRRIEMOOR (Runiciman)
Carrier	LEONIAN (United Africa)
Netlayer	MINSTER (Southern Railway)
Netlayer	RINGWOOD (Southern Railway)

Hospital Carriers

    BATAVIER II

*   DINARD

    DUKE OF LANCASTER

    DUKE OF ROTHSAY

    ISLE OF JERSEY

*   LADY CONNAUGHT

*   NAUSHON

    NEW BEDFORD

*   PRAGUE

*   ST JULIEN (mined)

\#   EL NIL

\#   LLANDOVERY CASTLE

*** Br crew, US medics for US beaches**

\# Hospital ships, not used

<u>Additional Code Numbers allocated</u>

RD417   EMPIRE TWEED (x Gambian)

RD418   EMPIRE MERGANSER (US ww1)

Buoy Tenders, Cable, Survey & Light ships.

    ALERT (Trinity House Buoy Tender) +

    ALERT (Post Office Cable Ship)

    ANDRE BLONDEL (Fr Buoy Tender)

    DISCOVERY II (Br Antarctic Survey)

    EMPIRE FLAMINIAN (MOWT Cable)

    GEPRGES DE JOLI (Fr Buoy Tender)

    IRIS (Post Office Cable Ship)

    JUNO (Trinity House Lightship)

    KANSAS (Trinity House Lightship)

    LESLIE (Cable barge Port en Bessin)

    MONARCH (Post Office Cable Ship)

    PATRICIA (Trinity House Buoy Tender)

    NORMAN (Cable barge, engine trouble)

    WARDEN (Trinity House Buoy Tender)

US Tugs V4-M-A1

    BLACK ROCK

    BODIE ISLAND

    FARALLON

    GAY HEAD

    GREAT ISAAC

    HILLSBORO INLET

    MOOSE PEAK

    SABINE PASS

    SANKATY HEAD

    TRINIDAD HEAD

US MT Liberties & others

    A. FRANK LEVER

219   ABIEL FOSTER

    ALCOA TRADER

222   AMOS G. THROOP

248   ARTHUR SEWALL

    BELVA LOCKWOOD

218   BENJAMIN HAWKINS

    BERING

224   CLARA BARTON

236	HORACE GRAY	207	JOHN STEELE
	HORACE WILLIAMS		JOSEPH A. BROWN
	HUTCHINSON I. CONE		JOSEPH E. JOHNSTON
MT23	IGNATIUS DONNELLY		JOSEPH PULITZER
254	J. D. ROSS		JOSEPH STORY
	J. E. B. STUART		JOSHUA B. LIPPINCOTT
	J. WARREN KEIFER	229	JOSIAH NELSON CUSHING
	JAMES A. FARRELL		JUAN FLACO BROWN
241	JAMES B. WEAVER		JULIUS ROSENWALD
	JAMES CALDWELL	MT15	LEE S. OVERMAN
244	JAMES I. MCKAY		LEWIS MORRIS
255	JAMES L. ACKERSON		LOU GEHRIG
	JAMES R. RANDALL	204	LOUIS KOSSUTH
	JAMES WOODROW		LOUIS MARSHALL
	JANE G. SWISSHELM	239	LUCIEN B. MAXWELL
	JANE LONG		LUCIUS Q.C. LAMAR
228	JEDEDIAH S. SMITH	238	LUCY STONE
	JEREMIAH O'BRIEN		LYMAN HALL
246	JESSE APPLEGATE	MT17	MATTHEW T. GOLDSBORO
249	JIM BRIDGER		MELVILLE JACOBY
	JOHN A. CAMPBELL		MEXICAN
MT22	JOHN A. SUTTER		OLIVER EVANS
	JOHN A. TREUTLEN	214	OLIVER WOLCOTT
MT19	JOHN E. SWEET		OMAR E. CHAPMAN
MT31	JOHN E. WARD		OWEN WISTER
	JOHN F. STEFFEN		PANAMAN
	JOHN G. WHITTIER	MT17	PARK BENJAMIN

A further 61 cargo ships were assigned and loaded for Normandy, but were not dispatched until after the official end of Operation Neptune - 30 June in the British sector and 3 July in the US sector. They included 13 British and one Greek, the balance being US flagged Liberties.

Other tugs that may well have been involved include:

Abeilles 3, 6, 14, 16; Alliance, Aube [Fr], *Bustler, Cherburgoise 1, Danube V, Danube VI, Director, Diversion, Empire Alfred, Empire Ben, Empire Harry, Empire Imp, Empire Jane, Empire Jean, Empire Mary, Empire Nicholas. Empire Polly, Empire Sandy, Empire Sprite, Empire Susan, Empire Vincent, Enchanter, Encore, Enigma, Enticer, Gatteville* [Fr], *Isere* [Fr], *Justice, Marauder, Mastodonte* [Fr], *Nancy Moran, Nessus* [Fr], *Palencia,* HMS *Reward, Richard Lee Barber, Sun XII, Zeeleeuwe.* Plus an unknown number of TID tugs

Notes:

Some of the ships listed as British were from other European nations, many with part British manning.

Where coasters are marked US they are mostly Dutch Schuyts in US service, usually with some British crew.

Sources:

Documents at The National Archives, John de S. Winser's D-Day Ships, Willem Holdenburg and others; cross checked with Lloyd's Registers from the Plimsoll website and Talbot-Booth's Merchant Ships 1943.

Dry Cargo Coasters (sector)	463 (includes 20+ Dutch schuyts for US sector)
Coastal Colliers	11
Coastal Tankers	61
Salvage Vessels	26
Lifting Craft	9 (non-propelled)
Pump Vessels	20 (most were employed on the UK coast)
Military Transports	112
MOWT LSIs and troopers	40
MOWT tugs	50
Deep Sea Tankers	13 (+ one RFA, one more stayed in UK)
Hospital Carriers	12 (includes 2 Hospital Ships, not used)
Accommodation Vessels	7
Block ships	32
Total	**856**

Index

9 780955 744150